To Jan
a great p
thank yw of
Jonathan

THE WELSH WARRIOR
THROUGH THE AGES

By

Jonathan Morgan

Published in the United Kingdom in 2016 by

Cambria Books, Wales, United Kingdom.

Website: www.cambriabooks.co.uk

Illustrations by Robert Macdonald RWSW (President), MA (RCA), Diop.LCSAD.

Cover design by Carolyn Michel.

Thanks and Acknowledgements:

Col Nick Lock of the Royal Welsh for his essay on the Royal Welch Fusiliers in Bosnia

Syd Morgan for his essay on General Lloyd

Alun Jones for his proof reading

Frances Chaffey for secretarial and typewriting

St Loye's Foundation

The R S Thomas Estate

The following for sponsorship:

Lord Ashcroft

Dan Clayton-Jones

Geraint Williams

Mitchell and Meredith

Kirsty Williams AM

Chris and Annette Thomas

Jonathan Arter

Guy Clarke OBA

The Gibbs Trust

Cardiff Metropolitan University

Peter Thomas, Chairman of Cardiff Blues

Gwyn Williams

Royal Welsh Brecon Branch

Sheila and Peter Jenkins of Brecon Car Sales

Nicholas Morgan

Julie Bell of The Griffin, Felinfach

Richard Wyatt

Trefor Evans

Peter Brooke

The Dowlais British Legion

Roger Williams

Lady Sue Large

J Js

Wyn Wormsley

Regimental Association of the Royal Welsh

Aberystwyth University

ABOUT THE AUTHOR

Jonathan Morgan was educated at Christ College, Brecon, R.M.A. Sandhurst, and Aberystwyth, Cardiff and Glamorgan Universities. He also taught at U.W.I.C. (now Cardiff Metropolitan) for nine years. Jonathan's father the Rev. G Rex Morgan, Chaplain to the King's Royal Rifle Corps and Senior Housemaster at Christ College, Brecon, was a well-known prisoner-of-war and was on the dreadful 'Shoe Leather Express' March in Poland. It is interesting that Christ College former pupils won 23 MCs in the First World War.

Jonathan's was a great Welsh sporting family which included Guy Morgan, Captain of Cambridge University and Wales at rugby and Glamorgan at Cricket, and Dr. Teddy Morgan, Captain of Wales and the British Lions at rugby. Rex's cousin Guy (not the rugby player), was a Royal Navy Lieutenant and prisoner-of-war who wrote the well-known play 'Albert R.N.'. Jonathan's mother, Glenys, was the daughter of Captain T.L.Morgan, Adjutant of the 15th Welsh in the early part of the Great War.

As well as a sportsman himself, Jonathan is a 3rd Order Anglican Franciscan. He was invalided out of the Army with PTSD or related illness in 1980 and had served with the Royal Regiment of Wales as a Captain which included an horrific tour of Northern Ireland in the Ardoyne and Bone district of Belfast.

ABOUT THE ILLUSTRATOR

Robert Macdonald, an artist who lives near Brecon, is a past Chair of the Welsh Group, the senior association of professional artists in Wales, and President of the Royal Watercolour Society of Wales. He is a graduate of the Royal College of Art. Born in 1935, his childhood was shaped by the upheavals of the Second World War. After losing their home in a wartime bombing raid the Macdonalds emigrated to New Zealand in 1945. Robert did military service in the New Zealand Army.

He returned to Britain in 1958 and studied at the London Central School of Art. Since coming to live in Wales with his Welsh-born wife Annie he has been inspired by the Welsh landscape and mythology.

CONTENTS

Foreword by Lord Ashcroft KCMG PC

The opening verse of the Welsh National Anthem, Land of My Fathers, leaves nobody in any doubt that the Welsh are a proud people who greatly value courage: "Her brave warriors, patriots, For freedom shed their blood." ("Ei gwrol ryfelwyr, gwladgarwyr tra mad, Dros ryddid collasant eu gwaed.")

As a champion of bravery and an enthusiastic collector of gallantry medals for the past 30 years, I am well aware that time and again Welsh servicemen have displayed immense courage in battle. Scores of men with strong Welsh links have been awarded the Victoria Cross (VC), Britain and the Commonwealth's most prestigious gallantry medal and awarded for courage in the face of the enemy. Medals awarded to Welshmen form a significant part of my VC collection, currently nearing 200 strong and the largest of its kind in the world.

I feel privileged to be the custodian of so many VCs awarded to courageous Welshman: among the VCs that I treasure is the award to Private Robert Jones, from Monmouthshire, who took part in the famous defence of Rorke's Drift in South Africa in 1879. Jones' wonderful gallantry and unfortunate death are well documented in this book.

The VC, which is 160 years old, is awarded 'For Valour' and there is no doubt that Welshmen have, over the centuries, displayed valour in spades. It is for this reason

1

that The Welsh Warrior Through The Ages is both an inspirational title and a long-overdue book.

The Welsh are said to have been England's earliest ally because Welsh archers fought with Edward 1 against the Scots. Over the centuries, during times of war and conflict, the nation's servicemen have played vital roles in the Army, the Royal Navy and the RAF, never more so that during the two world wars.

In recent years, Jonathan Morgan has established his credentials as a talented writer, historian and essayist. He has put an immense amount of work into his latest book and I commend it to one and all. The Welsh Warrior Through The Ages is a labour of love that will be enjoyed and cherished for many decades to come.

Lord Ashcroft KCMG PC is a businessman, philanthropist, author and pollster. For more information on his work and his role in championing bravery, visit www.lordashcroft.com. Follow him on Twitter: @LordAshcroft

WELSH HISTORY

By Ronald Stuart Thomas

We were a people taut for war; the hills
Were no harder, the thin grass
Clothed them more warmly than the coarse
Shirts our small bones.
We fought, and were always in retreat,
Like snow thawing upon the slopes
Of Mynydd Mawr; and yet the stranger
Never found our ultimate stand
In the thick woods, declaiming verse
To the sharp prompting of the harp.
Our kings died, or they were slain
By the old treachery at the ford.
Our bards perished, driven from the halls
Of nobles by the thorn and bramble.
We were a people bred on legends,
Warming our hands at the red past.
The great were ashamed of our loose rags
Clinging stubbornly to the proud tree
Of blood and birth, our lean bellies

And mud houses were a proof
Of our ineptitude for life.
We were a people wasting ourselves
In fruitless battles for our masters,
In lands to which we had no claim,
With men for whom we felt no hatred.
We were a people, and are so yet.
When we have finished quarrelling for crumbs
Under the table, or gnawing the bones
Of a dead culture, we will arise
And greet each other in a new dawn.

Ronald Stuart Thomas

From the Collected Poems of R S Thomas 1945-1990, first published in Great Britain 1993 by J M Dent, The Orion Publishing Group. Permission has been granted by R S Thomas' estate to include this poem.

INTRODUCTION

It is probably a fact of history that, when a small country stands as an adjunct of a big, powerful country, the collective unconscious or psyche of that small country probably has the characteristics of an inferiority complex. In terms of the Welsh, the defeat and demise of both Prince Llewelyn and Owain Glyndwr have probably given them the role of victim or glory in defeat.

Regarding military prowess, it has been perceived that the Celts have sometimes been used as cannon fodder, coming from small impoverished countries while the British Army is run primarily by the English establishment who have wound up the Celts to prove themselves in battle. Hence the huge proliferation of gallantry awards acquired by the Celts.

The difference in some ways between the Welsh and the Scots and the Irish is that at the Battle of Bosworth in 1485 Henry Tudor, a self- acclaimed Welshman led a primarily Welsh army to defeat the English King Richard III and his army.

The Irish were terrorised partly by the Welsh in that Elizabeth Tudor put some of the Scots settlers into Ireland. Oliver Cromwell came from a Welsh brewing family called Morgan Williams who changed their name to Cromwell to curry favour with their powerful maternal uncle Thomas Cromwell in Henry VIII's reign.

Latterly, it was Lloyd George who was instrumental in putting the dreaded Black and Tans into Ireland. The Scots had the tradition especially in the Highlands of following the Pretenders, and they were defeated by the English. The Welsh therefore, certainly, should not have an inferiority complex.

It was Elizabeth I (Tudor) who, having founded the first colony of Virginia, said to her great Welsh philosopher Dr John Dee, 'What shall we call this new empire?'

He said, 'Ma'am, you and I are the old British. We shall call it the British Empire, not the English Empire.'

The Welsh, like the Irish, have been great warriors and this book is a series of essays which praises their valour. There are themes that run through the book, one that is of chivalry started by the great King Arthur and which goes through many of the soldiers especially those in the Royal Welch Fusiliers with their great tradition of the war poets continued to this day by artists such as Sir Kyffin Williams, Major General Morgan Llewelyn and his son Glyn.

There have been exceptions of course, notably Captain Sir Thomas Picton who was a very cruel governor of Trinidad. There were great men like Lawrence of Arabia who attended the Welsh college of Jesus in Oxford, which was founded by a Welsh butcher's son, Hugh Price.

Wales is England's oldest ally; the Welsh archers fought with Edward I against the Scots. The archers were one of the great weapons of the English monarchy and won so many battles against the French. Today we celebrate 600 years since the Battle of Agincourt was fought, where 500 archers from Wales supported Henry V.

The Welsh have made their contribution in the navy over the years, and it is said that there were proportionally more Welshmen at Trafalgar than Englishmen. We all love freedom, but the Welsh, in particular, have nailed their colours to that mast.

Thomas Jefferson

Of the first six presidents of the United States, five had Welsh roots, and Jefferson, who wrote the Declaration of Independence said that his family were originally from the slopes of Snowden. A third of those who signed the Declaration were of Welsh stock, and the Welsh were highly instrumental in leading the rebellion against the English crown.

Again, many Welshmen from mining families went to fight on the Republican side in the Spanish Civil War against the forces of Fascism. Also, men like General Rees fought against the onslaught of the Japanese in Burma. Rorke's Drift is incredibly famous, although only 30% of the British were from Wales, and only three of the VC's were Welsh.

In the First World War, Wales contributed more volunteers proportionately than any other part of the United Kingdom. There were many Welsh aces in the RAF.

Field Marshall Lord Charles Llewelyn Guthrie

The Welsh Guards had come off public duties before being sent to the Falklands, and were criticised there for their lack of fitness and they suffered awful casualties on the Sir Galahad. But in Iraq and Afghanistan they more than compensated for the down period of the Falklands and proved themselves one of the British army's finest regiments. Again, the Welsh Guards have contributed a disproportionate number of senior officers which culminated in the appointment of Charles Llewelyn Guthrie as chief of the general staff and field marshal.

There is no doubt that the Welsh in particular have found it difficult to attain to the highest ranks in the army, partly because in Victorian times, the Scots were more fashionable and in greater numbers. Kitchener seemed to have a down against senior Welsh officers, but this was partly because he disliked Lloyd George and thought that he was promoting some of his Welsh cronies to senior positions.

The fact is that many general officers from Wales have had VCs or MCs, which has given them the confidence to command a predominately English army.

Another theme that runs through the book is that of the trickster. Henry Tudor was described by Elton as devious, sly and fey. The tricksters start with Merlin, go on to Fluellen in Shakespeare's Henry V, Dr John Dee in the reign of Elizabeth I and most of all, Lloyd George. This is an element of the Celtic twilight area that the English have never been able to understand. They think that we are sometimes 'with the fairies', and I remember in my own regiment the Royal Regiment of Wales, Captain Tony Asquith asking me, 'How all that darkness was down in Wales'. Having now read Henry Vaughan, the great Welsh metaphysical poet, I would say to him, 'Do you mean the dazzling darkness?'

The Welsh have fought all over the world, epitomised by Major General Humphrey Evans Lloyd who fought for the French against the Austrians, the Jacobite forces of Charles Stuart against the British, the Austrians against the Prussians and the Prussians against the Austrians, also the Russians against the Turks. The Welsh have been great fighters and are still an integral part of the British Army, defenders of the faith and the United Kingdom.

It is probably in Victorian times that the idea came about that there should be in Celtic regiments a preponderance of English public schoolboys in command. The balance has changed, and certainly in Wales, where 95% of the population go to comprehensive schools, we would deny ourselves access to a huge resource of talent if we carried on in this way. Also, if many of the officers are English and most of the men Welsh, it does give the Welsh a slight feeling of inferiority.

Finally, we must remember that the majority of warriors are not officers but the men, and I am reminded of a story a Second World War veteran told me that when the commanding officer of the Royal Welch Fusiliers addressed the regiment he announced, 'Gentlemen of the Royal Welch Fusiliers and men of other regiments'.

In modern times, the Royal Welch Fusiliers distinguished themselves particularly in the Bosnian conflict where their performance at Gorazde in particular led to a number of gallantry medals. This episode has been covered comprehensively in the book, 'The White Dragon' by Lt Col Jonathan Riley. The RWF still have that sense of the artistic about them. The Reverend Major

General Morgan Llewelyn, who was commanding officer of the regiment is an artist and his son Glyn is interested in poetry. However, not all the Welsh warriors were so good; Black Vaughan is the name given to the spectre of one of the old Lords who was so evil that his ghost was condemned to roam Hergest Court House and its lands for all eternity.

The Vaughans possessed the house for most of its history, and Black Vaughan is supposed to be the ghost of Sir Thomas who was killed in 1469. He is said to appear in various forms, including that of a bull. He roamed the nearby countryside terrifying women by leaping onto their coaches as they rode home. He is also said to have left physical impressions in the ground after his visitation in the form of bare patches of grass.

Similarly, a black dog is said to accompany him or roam the grounds by itself. It is said to be the spirit of Sir Thomas's favourite hound. In fact, Arthur Conan Doyle himself stayed at the hall as a guest of a later generation of the Vaughans and it is commonly believed that the story of the ghostly dog served as the inspiration for 'The Hound of the Baskervilles'. According to legend, Black Vaughan was actually laid to rest by a team of 12 people carrying crucifixes and oddly, a new born baby. Reading passages from the Bible, and praying fervently they are said to have laid his spirit to rest.

There was another evil man known as 'Black Herbert' who was of the famous Herbert family; Sir William ap Thomas was knighted by King Henry VI and became known to his compatriots as Y Marchog Glas o Gwent (The Blue Knight of Gwent) because of the colour of his armour.

William ap Thomas's son was known as 'Black Herbert' partly because of his villainy and partly because he sported a great black beard.

As well as the theme of magic that runs through the book, there is also one of treachery when Lancelot betrays Arthur by his intrigue with Guinevere and when Mordred is said to have stabbed Arthur fatally at the Battle of Camlan. Also, when many of the Welsh archers helped to slit the throats of the French prisoners at Agincourt, here was another example of brutality. It was not all chivalry, although the Celtic tradition does reinforce chivalry which continues to this day in the Welsh regiments.

It is significant, the author believes, that, when he received Lady Thatcher's letter saying that her family did not originate from Wales, and John Campbell says in his book that her father's side of the family came originally from Wales, there is a thought that certain people, especially in the English establishment feel it is downmarket to come from Wales. It is interesting that the Welsh Guards carried Lady Thatcher's coffin.

King Arthur

KING ARTHUR AND MERLIN

The whole concept of King Arthur and his court was based, for the most part, on Geoffrey of Monmouth's *Historia Regum Britannie* which survives in 200 manuscripts. Geoffrey of Monmouth was a Welsh or Breton monk born in Monmouth, and he located Arthur's Camelot in the city of Caerleon built out of Roman remains.

Although much is mythical in his writing, as with the story of Jesus Christ, there is no smoke without fire. In the book, 'The Holy Kingdom', Adrian Gilbert goes into much research which talks about Arthur as a king coming out of Glamorgan.

There seem to be two main strands in the historicity of Arthur, the first being that he was a great leader emerging from the Roman exit from Britain. Another strand says he was originally a Welsh chieftain who held back the Saxon expansion. His greatest battle was The Battle of Badon which Geoffrey sites at Bath. Here, Arthur won a great victory.

He was said to have been the son of Arthur Pendragon and Igerna, the beautiful chaste wife of Gorlinas and Geoffrey claimed he was born at Tintagel, a place of huge romance. His intimate advisor was Merlin, who Count Tolstoy says originally hailed from the still Celtic area of

Northumberland. Geoffrey had found a Welsh legend of a seer called Myrddin (Merlin).

Merlin's concept came from a long line of what many people would call Shamans, and traditionally the Celtic princes always had a counsellor. Merlin fitted this bill and comes from the view of the Celts as possessing psychic powers. In terms of chivalry, the Round Table first appears in Wace's 'Roman de Brut', a Norman language adaption of Geoffreys' book. He says Arthur created the Round Table to prevent quarrels among the barons, none of whom would accept a lower place than the others.

Wace claims that the source of the Round Table legend came from the Bretons, and the table was certainly a custom recorded in many Celtic stories in which warriors sat in a circle around the King. During the Middle Ages, festivals called Round Tables were celebrated throughout Europe, in imitation of Arthur's court.

In Robert de Borons' 'Merlin', written around the 1190's, the wizard Merlin creates the Round Table as a copy of the table of the Last Supper and of Joseph of Arimathea's Holy Grail. One empty place is kept to mark the betrayal of Judas. The story of Percival says this seat must remain empty until the coming of the knight who will retrieve the Grail.

The Grail, again traditionally, has a number of interpretations including that of the vessel that caught the blood of Christ when he was dying on the cross. Another thread is that it was the receptacle of the wine handed out by Jesus in the Last Supper.

In Welsh terms, the Grail was brought by Joseph of Arimathea and ended up at Strata Florida Abbey, and, after the closure of the Abbey, it was put in the hands of its guardians the Powells of Nanteos. It was a wooden receptacle which many people used to come and drink water out of in the house in the beautiful valley outside Aberystwyth in which Nanteos stands.

The tragedy today is that it was recently stolen from the farmhouse of the Murleys, descendants of the Powells in Herefordshire. It was, however, returned some time later after a reward was offered, and will now be on permanent display at the National Library of Wales in Aberystwyth.

The quest for the Holy Grail is one of the great concepts of European history.

Carl Gustav Jung likened it to a journey which culminated in a completion of the individual attaining wholeness or holiness.

It is a quest that still goes on, with people travelling to the farthest corners of the earth, and in the future into space on this epic search.

Merlin's Oak was traditionally associated with Carmarthen, and it was claimed that the origin of the name Carmarthen or Caerfyrddin comes from Myrddin, the Welsh name for Merlin. Merlin is said to have made a prophecy regarding the old oak tree, 'When Merlin's oak shall tumble down, then shall fall Carmarthen town.' However, it reality, it was probably planted by a schoolmaster in 1660 to celebrate the return of King Charles II to the throne of England.

In the early 19th century a local man appears to have poisoned the tree with the intention of stopping people meeting under it, and it was believed to have died in 1856.

Guinevere is first named as Arthur's queen in the 'Culhwch and Olwen' tale from the Mabinogion, written down in the c11th but passed down orally from the c6th.

Legend has it that Guinevere and Lancelot were lovers, and cheated on Arthur.

The Arthur story was one very much identified with the Celts and especially those of Wales.

The most terrible battle was the final one in which treachery won the day. It was the fatal battle of Camlan, where his nephew Mordredd tried to usurp Arthur's throne. Both Arthur and Mordredd were killed. There is a large literature that refers to the dying Arthur being carried in a boat to his resting place. Some say this is to Bardsey Island, the island of the Saints; others to Glastonbury across the Marshes.

Graves were found at Glastonbury but never identified. Adrian Gilbert locates Arthur's grave in the Vale of Glamorgan. These stories are the ones that give rise to the tradition of chivalry in Celtic culture. They were attached to other traditions of the Celts going berserk in battle, either fuelled by drug-producing plants as were the Druids in their suicide fight against the Romans, or maybe it was a psychic phenomenon.

It is interesting, that in latter ages, many Welshmen achieved huge acts of courage in battle, not of course, drug induced but maybe there is something in the Celtic psyche which arouses men and women to furious heights of combat.

Henry Tudor or Henry VII realised the importance of the Arthurian tradition by calling his eldest son Arthur, and it was he who, after the Battle of Bosworth,

18

established the Yeoman of the Guard, the King's bodyguard - some would say the oldest British regiment. A Welsh line was again on the throne of Britain.

The Arthurian Tradition. John Matthews, Element Books Ltd, 1994

The Grail, The Quest for a Legend. Andrew Sinclair, Sutton Publishing, Gloucester, 2007

Y Seint Greal, The Holy Greal. Robert Williams, Jones Publishers, Wales, 1987

The Quest for Merlin. Nikolai Tolstoy, Hamish Hamilton, London 1985

King Arthur, History and Legend. J & C Matthews, The Folio Society, London 2008

The Legacy of King Arthur. Barber & Pykitt, Blorenge Books, Monmouthshire, 2005

The Lord Rhys

THE LORD RHYS AND LADY GWENLLIAN

One of the greatest heroines of Wales was Gwenllian, daughter of the warrior king of Gwynedd, Gryfydd ap Cynan. She fell in love with Grufydd ap Rhys. His father Rhys ap Tudwr was the last king of Deheubarth.

Henry I was on the throne of England, and he was determined to capture and kill the rebellious Grufydd. A plot to kill the latter had failed, and Grufydd went into a hiding place in the forests of Ystrad Tawy.

Grufydd led a rebellion and just before, Gwenllian had joined him in the forest. Their youngest son, who became the Lord Rhys was born in 1132.

In 1121, Henry invaded Wales but Grufydd kept very quiet and was allowed to live peaceably at Dinefor Castle. Henry again fell out with him, and the Welshman waged guerrilla war against the Normans.

Henry died in 1135, and the kingdom was wracked by division and rebellion. After New Year's Day 1136, while her husband was away, the Normans attacked Grufydd's possessions in SW Wales.

Gwenllian led the Welsh army against the Normans. Despite her evasive tactics, her army was caught between two Norman attacks. Her son Morgan of 18 years, was killed at her side. Gwenllian was captured, and, despite pleading for mercy, was executed over the body of her son. Her son, Rhys, was only 4 at the time, but there was partial revenge when her husband defeated the Normans in a battle at Cardigan a year later.

It is very interesting that certainly one scholar, Dr Andrew Breeze believes that she was the author of 'The Four Branches of the Mabinogion'.

Rhys was in many ways one of the great successes of Welsh history at this time. There was a limited number of chronicles engaged in Welsh historical writing, but Rhys was so important that he attracted the attention of many outside Wales.

At the tender age of 5, Rhys had lost his parents. There is no doubt that the nobles of the time lived according to strict codes of honour, although aggression was often required to survive.

He was 14 years old when first mentioned in the chronicles, fighting alongside his brothers when they captured the castle of Llansteffan. Rhys worked closely with his brother Maredudd, and they achieved much success. He was soon left as the sole representative of the southern dynasty based at Dinefor.

For the years 1155 to 1171, he was involved in total struggle to maintain the Deheubarth territory, and it was his misfortune to take control of it when the formidable King Henry II took the throne of England. Rhys listened to wise counsel, and took advantage of safe conduct to start engaging Henry II in diplomatic manoeuvres.

There were times, especially when the king was absent in France, when Rhys took advantage of Henry's absence in France.   Rhys in many ways accepted Henry's overlordship, and although he argued, he held his land not by gift or grant of the King, but by right and freely.

Further rebellion occurred, and by the end of 1164 the Welsh had overrun Ceredigion and its castles. Henry tried a couple of times to conquer Wales, but, partly owing to the hostility of the weather, was forced to withdraw.

The king's adventures in Ireland rather took his eye off Wales. Rhys wisely was tactfully and strategically diplomatic with the king, and even helped to supply the king's expedition to Ireland.

In fact, in the years around 1174, when Henry was faced by a formidable coalition of enemies, Rhys himself led a strong force of Welshmen to assist in the siege of a rebel stronghold.

It was around this time when the crisis was over for Henry that the Anglo Norman Marcher Lords took oaths of allegiance to the king, and some of them settled old scores. William de Braose, Lord of Brecon, Abergavenny, Builth and Radnor invited his neighbour Seisyll ap Dyfnwal, Lord of Upper Gwent, to dine at Abergavenny Castle.

Although Braos was conspicuous by his absence, his uncle Phillip and associate Ranolph Poer Sheriff of Hereford arranged the murder of the disarmed Welsh at dinner and saw that the dirty deed was done. The Seisylls could well be the same family that later came to prominence in Tudor times.

The Lord Rhys was said by the poet Cynddelw Brydydd Mawr that:

'He who likes to sing the work of poets himself is a leader of men, a brave lord

A man of whom England is afraid

He is a leader for this country,

A giant, a new warrior.'

He goes on to say,

'In battle in arms

He makes dust of armies, he is like to a shield in battle

I know his anger full well

I have fought with him in battles and we have made peace with the enemy together.

I will praise him as a soldier till I die'

Rhys was one of the foremost Welsh rulers to erect castles and appreciate their strategic significance. Cardigan Castle was one of his first recorded fortresses. He was a first class statesman, and by his diplomacy kept the English at bay. He was very generous to the monasteries of Strata Florida , Cardigan and Llandovery and was close to the Cistercians.

The title that eventually was accredited to him was The Lord Rhys, or Arglwydd Rhys, but this was probably given to him retrospectively. He was also responsible for much of the law making that consolidated Hywel Dda and the codification of Welsh law.

He had a keen ear for music, patronised the poets and even sang himself. He really started the concept of Eisteddfod at Cardigan Castle, likened by many to the Eisteddfod of our own time, and it very much reflected what now takes place. The event was announced a year in advance and two chairs were given, one for music and one for poetry.

He was a man of many parts, and was very much a Welshman, although he adapted some of the traditions of the Normans.

Professor Sir R R Davies puts forward the idea of Rhys as a reformer. He is of the opinion that one of the qualities that marks Rhys out from his contemporaries was his ability to come to terms with the new, as well as to exalt the old.

The historian Rhoscomyl says that, though history may show you some places where the Lord Rhys went wrong, you will still believe he was great and that he is in the right place when he is set down as one of the standard bearers of Welsh history.

The Age of Conquest, Wales 1063-1415. R. R. Davies, Oxford University Press, 1997

The Lord Rhys. Roger Turvey, Gomer Press, 1996

Prince Llewelyn

PRINCE LLEWELYN

There is no doubt that Llewelyn ap Gruffudd was the first Prince in the history of Wales to secure the King of England's recognition of his title to a large part of the country. Only his grandfather Llewelyn ap Iorwerth or Llewelyn the Great had brought together such a large part of Wales.

Much of our understanding of what they did comes from the work of John Edward Lloyd, 'A History of Wales from the Earliest Times to the Edwardian Conquest'.

The King of England would have liked to control the Principality of Wales in so much that it wouldn't be a regular thorn in his side; however, Llewelyn ap Gruffudd was determined to preserve the integrity of the Welsh Kingdom. Here was a strategy on both sides of the principle of divide and rule.

Treachery is a common theme in Welsh history, and there is no doubt that Gruffudd's defeat at Bron Yr Erw was caused partly by the defection of the men of Llun. Betrayal was an ultimate theme because everyone likes to be on the winning side, and, if a Prince is perceived not to be on the winning side, his support drains away.

The Battle of Bryn Derwyn in June, 1250 was a turning point for Gwynedd when Llewelyn installed himself as its sole ruler after defeating his brothers. He gradually expanded his position into such areas as Dynefor and Carreg Cennen. His authority was extended through much of Wales and by 1260 he had taken in Buellt, driving out its Anglo Norman Lord Roger Mortimer. Henry III at this time was very much involved with the rebellion of Simon de Montfort which very much weakened his position.

In 1265, Simon was killed in battle against the Royalist forces at Evesham and Henry was restored to power. Henry proceeded to make a treaty with Llewelyn and although Llewelyn did homage to the King, he was granted the status of pre-eminent Welsh leader with Welsh lords and local dynasties formally subordinated to him.

The treaty was not without flaws; his lands and title were granted to him, but grants could be withdrawn. He had shown himself clever at creating alliances within Wales, and was a skilful military leader but the English were still in parts of mid and S.E. Wales and no specific border had been demarcated at the Treaty of Montgomery.

The Prince was committed to the protection of Welsh law, Welsh culture and Welsh independence but, at times, he was still undermined from within. After the death of Henry III in 1272, Edward I, a far more powerful personality took over in England and he insisted on Llewelyn's doing homage. Open conflict between Prince and King soon erupted. On 12th November, 1276, Edward declared Llewelyn a rebel and began preparations for war.

Edward, at the head of an army, marched from Chester and penetrated Gwynedd as far as Conwy. Llewelyn was forced to surrender, and on November 19th, 1277, the Treaty of Aberconwy was signed and Llewelyn's powers were heavily curtailed. Llewelyn was reduced to controlling a territory which he had controlled thirty years earlier, before his expansion.

From 1277 onwards, Edward operated as a formal overlord, interfering in Llewelyn's jurisdiction. Huge resentment began to build up in Wales at the arrogance of the Anglo-Normans, and rebellion broke out on 21st March, 1281. Edward's response was swift. Llewelyn found himself driven into Snowdonia, from whence he sought to move east towards the border.

Roger Mortimer had died in October, 1282 and Llewelyn moved towards Buellt, where he received promises of aid from Mortimer's kinsmen. The accusation of treachery fell particularly on the Marcher Lords. In the most explicit statement we have, the Hagnaby chronicler says that Edmund Mortimer, Roger's brother, beseeched Llewelyn to come to the neighbourhood of Buellt to take his homage. Roger le Strange was undoubtedly the person mainly responsible for the forces that confronted Llewelyn before Buellt.

The fullest account is by Walter of Guiseborough and it describes the Prince's descent from the mountains, to find out the men of the land who were still loyal to him. The main part of his army was on the main slopes of the Wye with a contingent guarding a bridge across the Irfon.

The English resorted to a ford upstream, outflanking the Welsh and the bridge was taken, Llewelyn heard the noise of combat and rushed to join his army but he was pursued by an English soldier who struck him a blow without recognising him and left him wounded.

There was bloody slaughter of the Welsh army and, after the battle, the soldier returned to the person whom he'd struck down earlier in the day. He now recognised him as the Prince of Wales, and his head was severed and sent to the King as a ghastly sign of triumph.

There was another story from the Hagnaby Chronicle which said that as the Prince's army was being destroyed, leaving Llewelyn alone with only one servant, they left the battlefield where two of their enemies came upon them and followed them to a wood. They were found and surrounded, and after a strenuous fight, the Prince fell, revealing his identity.

'Glory to God in the Highest, peace on earth and goodwill, a triumph to the English, victory to King Edward and to the Welsh everlasting extermination.' So wrote a clerk in Edward I 's service.

The Croes Nedd, a piece of the true cross which had been in the care of Llewelyn's dynasty, was handed over to the King of England.

Great castles were built by Edward and the Welsh were treated like aliens in their own land. Only the English were allowed to command positions and to live in the towns around Wales and the land surrounding the castles. Llewelyn was the last of the Princes of Wales, and the antecedent of the Investiture when Edward pronounced his son Prince of Wales and presented him on the battlements of Caernarfon.

A huge blow was inflicted on the psyche of the Welsh people, and a feeling of depression and simmering revenge took root, to be exploited later by Owain Glyndwr. Llewelyn had been a great warrior, but he found himself up against one of the greatest Anglo-Norman Kings, Edward I, a great warrior himself.

Sheer power, organisation and resources were to defeat him. Edward recognised the Welsh as a war-like race, and his soldiers and followers sheltered behind the magnificent castles to avoid the dangers of the Welsh outlands. Never again would Wales be totally independent, except for a fleeting time under Glyndwr. It is not until the present day that some power has been given to the Welsh to run their own country again.

Edward I was keen to break down the Welsh tribal system. He set up garrison towns and walls were built to encircle them. Charters were given to the townspeople who were English and the Welsh who remained in the vicinity of these new fortresses were driven to the hills.

The defeat of Llewelyn festered long in the Welsh psyche, and, even today, there is huge remorse that he was the last Prince of Wales and a gathering at Cilmeri every year is held to commemorate this. Even the Tudor victory did not seem to banish this slur on the collective psyche.

Llewelyn, Prince of Wales: Warrior of a Lost Nation. (People from the Past) 28 Nov 1977. Margaret Williams, Dobson Books

A History of Wales. John Davies, Allen Lane The Penguin Press 1993

The Matter of Wales. Jan Morris, Oxford University Press 1984

Welsh Archers

THE WELSH ARCHERS IN THE 100 YEARS WAR

Edward I, after his conquest of Wales found that he could recruit many Welshmen as soldiers for his frequent wars in Scotland and France. The speciality of the Welsh was their outstanding skill as archers. They used the longbow better than anyone else at this time.

Welsh archers served at the battle of Falkirk as early as 1298, and, from then onwards, were found in large numbers in the English armies of the 14th century.

There was a preponderance of Welsh archers at the battles of Crecy in 1346 and Poitiers 1456. The Red Dragon of Cadwallader, a Welsh hero of the 7th century became the recognised emblem of the Welsh.

When the Black Prince was thrown from his horse at Crecy, it was the dragon banner of Wales that was flung over him in protection while his enemies were beaten off. It was probably at Crecy that the leek became the Welshman's special badge when the Welsh men plucked leeks and wore them in their helmets, although this tradition is said to have gone back even as far as David's time.

The green and white of the Welsh banner may reflect the colour of the leek and certainly was associated with the royal colours of Wales. Prince Llewelyn was said to have been married in green and white. The colour was also associated with Cheshire and worn as probably the first uniforms of the Black Prince's archers as he was also Earl of Chester.

It is most interesting that in Brecon Cathedral's Heritage Centre there is a board on which are recorded the names of approximately 160 archers who went from the environs of Brecon to fight at Agincourt. The authenticity of the names is not questionable; they do fit in with the names recorded in *the Roll of Agincourt*. Although I have not checked every name, there is enough similarity to consider the board accurate. We do not know where the information came from but we suspect at one time it was in some sort of museum in America and was transferred to the Brecon Museum and thence to the Heritage Centre.

The archers from Wales who carried the longbow and used it with deadly accuracy were famous throughout Europe. There was certainly some foundation in the story that the longbow had originally come out of Wales. The Welsh bowmen of the Black Prince helped to win many battles and were considered highly disciplined and were some of the first infantry in Europe to wear uniform, the green and white colours of Wales.

Their dress was most interesting. They wore helmets and caps made of boiled leather. They wore sleeveless garments made of quilted coarse linen which resembled the padding on a modern fencing jacket.

When in action the shirt sleeves would be rolled and on the left forearm would be the leather brace (about 5" long) to take the impact of the bow string. They wore coarse homespun breeches gathered at the knee and soft leather jack boots of the kind we associate with Russian peasants (minus high heels). A small round target or shield was carried on the left side of the sword. A mace was often carried as a small side arm. Hanging from the belt, in front, to the right, was a small pouch for the archer's wax and odds and ends.

Arrows were carried in sheaves of about 12, loosely bound and slung on the back or thrust through the belt. During a battle further ammunition was supplied by special runners. The longbow was equal to the height of a man.

Archers also carried a pole or palisade (a stake about 11 feet long sharpened at both ends), these were set up fairly close together with one end embedded in the ground and the other pointing outward about the height of a horse's chest and they formed a good protection against cavalry charges.

There would be no issued uniform, although, certainly earlier in the French wars, the Welsh would wear green and white. It is probable that all the troops in the King's army at Agincourt wore on their back and chest the red cross of St George on a white field.

I have a letter from reader James Travers, National Archives, which gives a fascinating account of the archers at Agincourt, as follows:

There were certainly both Welsh and English archers present at Agincourt but to establish relative numbers from the surviving documents is problematic. To begin with the term 'archer' as it appears in early fifteenth century musters did not necessarily denote a longbowman. 'Archer' simply distinguished soldiers paid at a certain rate from men at arms paid at another. Their weapons varied.

The surviving retinue rolls only gave a partial view of the composition of Henry's force that would have included Irish and Burghandians as well as English and Welsh. Welsh archers are known, from a variety of sources, to have joined the expedition to France.

Among the most distinguished of these were Roger Vaughan of Bredwardine; Watkin Lloyd of the Lordship of Brecknock; and the renowned David Llewelyn, better known as Dafydd Gam.

Such lists of archers as we have suggest a preponderance of English names, but this raises further questions about rendering Welsh patronyms in official documents and the greater likelihood of certain social groups being more recorded than others.

Wales has a long tradition of archery going back to the mythological figure Gwrnerth Ergydlym who reputedly slew the largest boar in Britain with an arrow of straw.

In Welsh tradition, messengers calling warriors to battle rode through the land waving a strung bow, while the return of peace was announced by the same, unstrung. The earliest bow found in Britain is dated 2690 BC and is this a Celtic bow? It was over six feet long and a good deal taller than the archer who shot it. It is a powerful flat yew bow bound with leather thongs in an intricate criss-cross pattern.

A longbow is made of wood – as opposed to those composite bows found in other parts of the world – and its length is at least equal to the height of the user and may even be a little more. Its width and thickness are nearly equal. In this it contrasts with the flat bow where the width is appreciably greater than its thickness.

From the military point of view, the advantage of the longbow is its ability to shoot a heavy arrow to an adequate range - in the order of 200 yards. Weight is needed in the shaft to achieve the penetration of mail and armour.

Records suggest that the most popular wood for bows at the time was the local wych or wild elm. However, the qualities of the yew, particularly from trees growing on harsh upland ground, was found to be superior. The best yew grows under hard conditions where slow growth gives the wood a close grain. Bows are made from the main trunk of the tree and not from branches, unless they are very large. In bow manufacture a combination of the outer sapwood and the inner heartwood is essential.

The appropriate yews were felled between December and February when sap levels are down and were then seasoned in kitchens and suspended high up with the hams in the smoke blackened beams.

Another important source of good yew for bow making was the Spanish peninsula and a thriving trade developed with medieval Wales. Other woods such as ash were popular with the Welsh archers. The idea that yews were planted in churchyards to provide wood for bows is a popular fallacy. They were planted as a sombre evergreen suitable for the solemnity of such places.

Archery was an essential part of a man's life. From an early age boys were encouraged to shoot and would have grown up in a society where proficiency with the bow was a skill at which to shine.

Archery has interested our national psyche; even the notorious two fingered salute, offensive today, represented little more than a gesture of defiance in the face of the enemy who sliced off the first two fingers of any captured bowmen.

Having looked at the longbow and the archers, also having looked at the composition of the British force at Agincourt, we ought perhaps to look a little bit at the battle. It took place on 25 October, 1415 on St Crispin's Day.

Henry V's army of 9,000 men defeated a French army of at least four times that number. It was David Gam, the Welsh squire, who had raised a body of men from Breconshire who was sent on the eve of the battle by the King to explore the numbers of the enemy. He returned to make the well- known answer: 'Enough to be taken prisoners and enough to run away'.

Several attacks were made by the French, some of them almost succeeding in overrunning the King's kinsman Walter Llwyd. At that moment the archers using their axes and swords penetrated the gaps in the French ranks and the attackers were slaughtered or taken prisoner to a man.

David Gam, and despite popular myth, there was no evidence that he was knighted on the field, was the man who at Owain Glyndwr's first parliament at Machynlleth attempted to kill the Welsh patriot and broke his pledge to Glyndwr time after time.

The Welsh Quisling slew his kinsman, Richard Fawr, Lord of Slwch, in the High Street of Brecon and this caused him to flee from Wales and seek service with Harry of

Monmouth. We are not sure if he was called Gam because he squinted or because his legs were crooked. He was killed at Agincourt and probably buried there, although, it is rumoured many of his descendants were buried under the choir of the Chapel of Christ College, Brecon and we have a memorial to two of his descendants in Brecon Cathedral.

His family once lived in Newton Farm on the edge of Llanfaes in Brecon and there are still many of the Games family about. His descendants in the male line eventually adopted the surname Games. They were among the most prominent patrons of Welsh poetry in the fifteenth century.

Gwladys, Dafydd Gam's daughter, married successively Sir Roger Vaughan of Tretower, and Sir William ap Thomas of Raglan. Her son, by the latter marriage, was William, the first Herbert, Earl of Pembroke. I believe Sir Roger Vaughan, Gam's son-in-law who also fought at Agincourt, was killed and his image is in the top stained glass window of the south transept in the Cathedral. There is little else I can find out about him except that he was of the well-connected Vaughan family.

Among the Welsh at Agincourt, Harry of Monmouth – if Shakespeare is to be believed, counted himself as one, for to Fluellen's remark that, 'Welshmen did good service in a garden where Leeke did grow, wearing leeks in their Monmouth caps', the King replies, 'I wear it for a memorable honour for I am Welsh, you know, good countryman'.

The Welsh Archer. Jeremy Spencer, Warbow Wales

The Hundred Years War. Jonathan Sumption, Faber & Faber, 1990

The Hundred Years War, Trial by Fire. Jonathan Sumption, Faber & Faber, 2011

Shakespeare and Wales. Edited by W Maley and P Schwyzer, Ashgate Publishing England, 2010

Owain Glyndŵr

OWAIN GLYNDŴR

On both sides of his family, Owain Glyndŵr could claim to be descended from the Welsh Princes. His mother, for instance, was descended from the princes of Deheubarth. The most probable date of his birth was 1359. He was eventually sent to London to be an apprentice of the law at Inns of Court. After being a law student, he became a squire and soldier.

His earliest experience as a soldier was in 1384 when the great Welsh captain Sir Gregory Sais gathered his troops on the Scottish border. Throughout these years, in service in this way to the Crown, Owain gained wide experience and proved himself a dashing and courageous soldier.

The Welsh poets described him, '*In his attacks on the Scots, he drove them howling with fear, like wild goats and "his attacks were so furious and quick, that not a blade of grass or corn would grow in his tracks."*'

He married Margaret Hanmer, a daughter of the most famous Welsh judge of the time of Edward III. He lived in a lovely timber framed house called Sycarth which was often described as elegant and it was girded by a moat of shining water.

He was very much one of the Welsh gentry or 'Uchelwyr'. Owain was partly caught up in the strife between Richard II and Henry IV with Richard's deposition. Henry tried to extract even more heavy communal payments from his Welsh subjects, which stirred up the Welsh. Owain, meantime, had fallen into dispute with Lord Grey of Ruthin.

Owain found no help from the King's court. He was an unlikely rebel, over 40 years of age, a substantial landowner and a married man with a large family. On 16th September, 1400, he met with a group of friends and family, where afterwards he was proclaimed Prince of Wales.

The King made no effort to investigate and solve Welsh grievances, so the rebellion spread and when Parliament met in January and February of 1401, it was enacted that no Welsh man should acquire property or land, or hold office in the English boroughs in Wales. Any English person in Wales convicted at the suit of a Welsh person was to be tried only by English justices.

The King chose Henry Percy, the famous hotspur to put down the rising tide of the Welsh rebellion. Owain looked for new ways to add to his strength by negotiating with the King's other enemies, with for instance the King of Scotland and the lords of Ireland.

1402 was an excellent year for Owain. On 22nd June, he defeated a large English force at Brynglas, near the village of Pilleth. The King assembled a very large army in 1402 which marched on through Wales. Owain was hopelessly outnumbered, the English were defeated by the weather. This is partly why they thought, and we shall later see Shakespeare describing Owain as, 'A magician in *league with the powers of darkness'.* The English were bogged down in hostile territory, and harassed at every turn by raids and ambushes of the highly mobile, lightly armed Welsh. Parliament called for even more stringent measures against the Welsh and a proclamation of 1402 made it illegal for the English to trade with the Welsh.

In March 1403, Owain was faced with a new problem. The Prince of Wales, the future Henry V was appointed the King's Lieutenant in Wales. At that time also Hotspur turned his sword on Henry, as did Mortimer. The joining of the forces of Owain, Hotspur and Mortimer would probably have done for Henry IV, but Hotspur was defeated at Shrewsbury before he could join up with the Welsh and he himself was killed in action.

Prospects looked good for Owain in 1404, but for Henry they looked bleak. Owain had secured Caernarfon and Cardigan, and he now confidently called representatives in Machynlleth.

He began his negotiation with France. Owain sent his brother in law John Hanmer and his chancellor Gruffydd Young as his representatives to France, and in his letter to the French King Charles VI, he styled himself 'Prince of Wales' and a treaty was concluded on 14th July.

The year 1405 was one of mixed fortunes for the rebels; Owain himself suffered two severe setbacks in south east Wales, where Prince Henry and his lieutenants defeated the Welsh near Grosmont and in May, they suffered a greater defeat at Pwll Melyn.

Henry assembled a very large army in 1405, and a French force had reinforced Owain at this stage although by early 1406, the French had withdrawn. Before the end of 1406, Welsh confidence was on the wane. Owain had lost control of a great part of his outlying territories, the Gower, the Towy Valley and large parts of Cardiganshire.

In addition to the laity, many of the clergy had given Owain their support: Franciscan friars devoted to the memory of Richard II and a number of the abbots of Cistercian monasteries Strata Florida, Aberconwy and Caerleon. Although Owain did not have the financial resources that the English did, on occasion he was able to raise a force of as many as 8 or 10,000 troops.

Owain relied much on plunder, and in front of the invading English armies, he implemented 'scorched earth' policy. The fact that the Welsh put up such a great fight was partly due to his considerable ability as a military commander.

Guerrilla tactics were the order of the day, with lightning raids, rapid switches of direction and the avoidance of pitched battles. As well as being a military captain, he was also a statesman.

As the sun went down on his rebellion there was much treachery as many of the rebels changed sides. There were a number of Welsh men who had been bitterly opposed to Owain, like Dafydd Gam from Brecon who was later killed at Agincourt.

After 1405, Henry's fortunes greatly improved. Much of the internal strife in England had disappeared. Despite Owain's guerilla tactics, the natural lines of communication in Wales ran east and west and not north and south; it was difficult to unite it. Also, the English had the advantage of sea power, castles and superiority in numbers and arms.

From 1407 onwards, Owain began to realise there was to be no victory. He lost Aberystwyth and Harlech in the summer of 1408. His last major effort was a raid in 1410 on the Shropshire border, but he was defeated.

In 1412, Henry IV died and Henry V took over in England, offering a pardon to all the Welsh rebels including Owain if they agreed to submit, but he refused. He disappeared, and it is most likely, despite all the myths, that he went to his daughter Alice who had married John Scudamore, a squire who lived in the secluded manor of Monnington Straddle in the Golden Valley.

Three early sources give the date of his death as about the 20th or 21st September,1415. He left Wales in a ruined state; churches, mills and farm buildings, monasteries and manors had been destroyed. Far from bringing about greater political and legal freedom for the Welsh, it had brought down on their heads savage laws. One bard sang,

'Against the English burgesses of Flint

Henceforth will I abjure for good slavish Flint and all its brood

May hell and all its furnace fires undo its English folk and piper too

My prayer is may they perish all my curse on them and all their children fall'

Owain was inspired by something more than personal ambition. He fought for the hope of freedom and independence as prophesied by the bards. He underlined two essential emotions; 'The awareness of the Welsh that they were a separate people with a history and culture of their own. That they were entitled to dignity and consideration and not as a conquered race of inferior barbarians.' So said Sir Glanmor Williams.

For 15 years, in a Welsh population about one twelfth the size of England, he had kept the flame of rebellion alight. All his sons died childless. He was never betrayed by his own men. Gruffydd Lloyd the bard said,

'Battling in tournament

Shattering men's bodies and overthrowing a hundred

Silence is commanded for him

As he sits at table at the head of a goodly company

He will tolerate no disorder of injustice

A companion fit to mingle with earls.'

Owen Edwards maintained that central to Owain's greatness was his attempt to create out of the disorder a nation with settled institutions and high ideals.

Shakespeare depicts him as *'Calling up spirits from the vasty deep'*

He goes on to say,

'In faith he is a worthy gentleman

Exceedingly well read and profited

In strange concealments valiant as a lion

And wondrous affable and as bountiful

As mines of India'

He epitomises the spirit that was to produce eventually after many centuries, a Welsh Assembly in Cardiff and a host of Welsh institutions which have rebuilt our nationhood.

Dafydd Gam, the trickster, was the prototype for Shakespeare's Fluellen. Shakespeare never set a play in England without incorporating a significant Welsh element. It is Fluellen who assures his King, Henry V, *'that all the water in the Wye cannot wash your Majesty's Welsh plod out of your pody.'*

Another possible model for Fluellen was the celebrated Welsh soldier Roger Williams, who was knighted by the Earl of Leicester after the Battle of Zutphen in 1586.

Fluellen spoke mostly English and only a little Welsh. Fluellen is portrayed as a soldier full of bravado, but even if slightly fey and comic in a way, no-one ever questions his bravery.

The Welsh archer has become a figure of greatness in the mythology of the 100 Years war, and although Dafydd Gam is said to have killed his cousin in Brecon High Street and was later captured by Glyndwr, he picked the right side to fight for and as has often happened in Breconshire history, the inhabitants backed the winning side.

The story of Sir Roger Vaughan and Gam rescuing Henry V before Agincourt is probably an apocryphal one, and Professor Currie the great expert on Agincourt says she can't even prove that Sir Roger Vaughan was there. Although the proportion of Welsh archers to the English was much lower at Agincourt than at Crecy, the Welsh despite Portugal's claim, have been England's oldest ally.

It is strange that, especially in Victorian times, their accents and language were mocked by the English establishment.

Owen Glendower. John Cowper Powys, Pan Books, 1978

The Revolt of Owain Glyn Dŵr. R R Davies, Oxford University Press, 1997

The Last Prince, Wales Braveheart: Owain Glyndŵr. The Last Welsh Prince of Wales. Benjamin James Baillie, paperback, 2014

Owain Glyndŵr:Prince of Wales. Ian Skidmore, Christopher Davies Publishers, 1986

Admiral Hugh Evan Thomas

THE WELSH IN THE NAVY

In the debate on the closure of Pembroke and Rhosaeth dockyards, on December 11th, 1925 at the House of Commons, Lloyd George said, 'There is no part of the kingdom that in proportion to its population contributes more to the British Navy than Wales. Although we live in the mountains, our mountains are high enough for us to see the sea from almost any part of our little land, and there is the eternal fascination of the sea.

It is with the greatest difficulty in the world that farmers can keep their sons from going to sea. They can see the steamers and the sailing ships passing to and fro, and there is for these men the eternal attraction of what is beyond the horizon.'

It has been suggested that, in proportion of size to population, there were more Welshmen than Englishmen in the Merchant Navy during Queen Victoria's reign. Much speculation surrounds the legend that Prince Madoc of Gwynedd discovered America in 1170. However, there is little evidence for this, although a memorial commemorating his landing was erected on the shores of Mobile Bay by THE DAUGHTERS OF THE REVOLUTION.

Cabot's historic voyage to the mouth of St Lawrence was captained by another Welsh man, Edward Griffiths.

There seems little foundation that America was named after Richard ap Meric or Mameryk, a prominent Welsh merchant of Bristol. There is no doubt that Wales produced a disproportionate number of pirates of the Caribbean, including three of the most famous: Sir Henry Morgan whom we have an essay on in this book, Howell Davies and Black Bart Roberts.

Welshmen sailed with Drake, Blake and Nelson as well as with Cook, Franklin and Scott. There is too much information about the whole of Wales's achievement in the Royal Navy to write about in one essay. However, Trafalgar is an interesting case in point.

Nelson's immortal signal, 'England expects that every man will do his duty' was a slight insult to the Scots, Welsh and Irish who served at Trafalgar. About 620 Welshmen served in the battle, probably more, constituting 3 to 4 per cent of the fleet's manpower compared with about 9 per cent from Scotland and 25 per cent from Ireland. In fact, proportionate to population, there were more Welsh mariners at Trafalgar than English ones.

There were 30 Welshmen aboard HMS Victory, many of whom came from Pembrokeshire. The oldest Welshman at the Battle was quartermaster Peter George of Milford, age 56, aboard HMS Spartiate. The youngest were 12 year old William Wyn Eyton of Flintshire, who served on HMS Neptune with two 13 year olds on other ships, Thomas Thomas of Cardiff and Hoskins Brown of Kidwelly. There were a number of Welsh officers including Lewis Rotley, 2nd Lt of the Royal Marines aboard HMS Victory.

Many were wounded including 24 year old marine James Davies of Pembroke who was aboard the Belleisle, the most damaged ship in the British fleet. He lost his right leg below the knee. Philip Fisher of Chepstow served on the famous fighting ship Temeriere. Although Wales provided no Trafalgar captain, one Charles Tyler could certainly be termed an adopted Welshman and raised a family at Underdown in Pembroke.

In modern times, Wales has only produced 2 First Lords of the Admiralty, although it had produced 2 in the 300 years before George Hall who was ennobled as Viscount Hall of Cynon Valley and Jim Thomas, born in Llandeilo but MP for Hereford, who held the post from 1951 to 1956.

The only First Sea Lord from 1960 to 1963 was Caspar John, the son of the most famous Pembroke artist Augustus John. Although he had a direct way of speaking and a steely gaze, he loved parties, pubs and dressing up informally. He drove round in a battered old former London taxi and flew his own planes. He was one of the founding fathers of the Fleet Air Arm and largely responsible for bringing helicopters into the Royal Navy. Although John had great misgivings about the cost of the Polaris, he supported it publicly.

In the First World War, Admiral Hugh Evan Thomas was second in command at the Battle of Jutland; his family had settled at Lleyn Madoc near Llanwrtyd Wells for generations and had also acquired the Gnoll estate at Neath and Pencerrig near Builth Wells. Although he did not have great connections to get on in the navy, he was a close friend of Sir John Jellicoe, Commander-in-Chief of the Grand Fleet.

He was also very friendly at Dartmouth with Prince George, younger son of the Prince of Wales, the future

King George V. At the latter's insistence he commanded the Britannia Royal Naval College at Dartmouth. By 1915 he was entrusted with one of the Grand Fleet's plum posts as Commander of the 5th Battle Squadron, consisting of the Queen Elizabeth class battleship, the most modern and powerful. This command placed him under David Beatty, Jellicoe's great rival, which didn't help Evan Thomas's relations with the former.

At the Battle of Jutland, which was a stalemate, Evan Thomas's actions were called into question. At one stage he failed to use his initiative to support Beatty. In his defence, it could be said that by positioning his force between the battle cruisers and the high seas fleet while taking heavy damage, he saved Beatty's entire battle force from being destroyed.

In more recent times, Vice-Admiral Ewan Raikes from Breconshire was Flag Officer Submarines, and generally considered a very able and brave submarine commander. Other Welshmen of indeterminate distinction were Thomas Button of Walton, Glamorgan who commanded a ship blockading the Spanish held harbour of Kinsale in 1601.

He displayed considerable personal courage in his career generally, once even rowing back and forth under fire to inspire the besiegers attacking a rebel held Scots castle. However, he was infamous for levels of corruption which included harbouring a particularly unpleasant pirate on his ship, allowing the latter to escape in exchange for two chests of sugar.

Against the Armada in 1588, it was said that one Piers Griffith from Penrhyn commanded a ship from Beaumaris that joined Drake's fleet at Plymouth. The Vice Admiral

Sir William Wynter was Brecon-born and descended from a family that had been based in the county for a long time. Interestingly enough, David Gwyn served on the other side.

Despite Portugal's pretensions, since Edward I's reign, Wales has been England's oldest ally, and Welshmen have fought in the Royal Navy all the way through, many of them with distinction.

There are a number of Welshmen in the navy who were awarded Victoria Crosses including Lt Commander Stephen Beattie who received his medal for great gallantry and determination in the attack on St. Nazaire March 27th, 1940. As Commander of HMS Campbeltown he directed his ship while under intense fire from close range and in the full glare of many search lights he steered it into the lock gates, beaching and scuttling her into the correct position.

Another VC was Commander John Linton born in Malpas, Newport. From the outbreak of the Second World War he was constantly in command of submarines and inflicted great damage on the enemy. He sank one cruiser, one destroyer, one U boat, 28 supply ships and in his last year he spent 254 days at sea, submerged for nearly half the time and his ship was hunted 13 times and had 250 depth charges aimed at her.

The tonnage sunk by Linton was the second highest of any British submarine commander. In 1942, he achieved the unique record of firing one salvo of 3 torpedoes and sinking 3 enemy ships. This was the sort of men contributed by Wales to the Royal Navy.

Britannia's Dragon, a Naval History of Wales. J D
Davies, The History Press, 2013

Sir Rhys ap Thomas

HENRY TUDOR AND SIR RHYS AP THOMAS

Two months after Edmund Tudor's death on 28th January 1457, Margaret Beaufort herself barely 13 years old gave birth to a son, the future Henry VII in a tower at Pembroke Castle. Henry Tudor, though he was born in Wales, lived his early years there, was only partly Welsh by descent. Of his 4 grandparents, his paternal grandfather Owain Tudor alone was a full blooded Welshman.

His grandmother Catherine of Valois was a descendant of French kings and the rulers of Bavaria. His mother, Margaret Beaufort, was of mixed aristocratic descent but from her great grandfather John of Gaunt had inherited a claim to the English throne. Henry lived with his mother only a short time, for she married Henry Stafford some time before 1464.

As a child, Henry had a Welsh nurse, a woman called Joan, wife of Philip ap Hywel of Carmarthen whom he rewarded after he became King. But we cannot be sure how long he was under her care, nor how much Welsh, if any, she taught him.

In 1461 Pembroke Castle and Henry Tudor were captured by Yorkist troops led by William Lord Herbert. Henry seems to have remained with the Herberts for the next 9 years, partly at Pembroke but probably, for much of the time, at the family's main residence at Raglan.

He proved to be a remarkably intelligent young man and was honourably educated. He was surrounded in Raglan by some of the leading bards of the day. This connection with the poets he never forgot. Following the defeat of the Yorkists in 1469 and the death of Herbert, Henry came back under the care of his father's brother Jasper. He was to be the main influence for many years on his nephew.

It was not until he was about 14 or 15 that he was taken to France by Jasper. They sailed from Tenby in 1471. So from 1457 for 14 years he had been in Wales. There are a number of English historians who tried to say he was French, partly because the English cannot bear being defeated by a Welshman but his whole inclination was towards Wales and that is why he landed at Dale in Pembrokeshire in 1485.

He marched through the rough tracks of western mid Wales knowing that there he would get a princely welcome. The 8 day march was accompanied by much support in Wales and on 14th August mounted on a white charger and under the red dragon standard of Cadwallader he crossed the border into England half way between Welshpool and Shrewsbury.

In the lead up to the battle, it was said Richard had in the region of 12,000 men whereas Henry's was less than 5,000. The majority came from Wales.

It is interesting that the whole tenor of the battlefield at Bosworth plays down the Welshness of Henry VII and his Welsh troops. Even Sir William Stanley's men are called the Men of Cheshire whereas many of them were the miners and colliers of Flintshire.

In view of such a remarkable preponderance of Sir William's contingent, it is not unnatural that he should come in on Henry's side. G M Trevelyan says, 'A Welsh gentleman named Henry Tudor landed with a slender and untrustworthy force at Milford Haven on the coast of his native Wales. The racial enthusiasm of the Welsh for a descendent of their ancient princes, marching as Henry was careful to march, under the red dragon standard of Cadwallader, broke out into prophesy and song and enabled them to raise in little more than a week a small army of zealous supporters.'

One of his most valiant supporters was Sir Rhys ap Thomas, who it is said was present at Dale to greet and pay his respects and homage to Henry. However, on Henry's advance, Sir Rhys shadowed from a distance Henry's army and finally joined it. In the charge that Richard made on Henry, Sir Henry Brandon, Henry Tudor's standard bearer was killed and the standard of the red dragon was given to Rhys Fawr ap Meredydd of Hiraethog, a man of massive strength and stature, of a long and distinguished lineage and according to local tradition Richard III was slain by Rhys Fawr.

It has been said Richard was slain by Sir Rhys ap Thomas but we shall probably never know the truth. It is said that Henry himself never forgot his Welsh blood or the services which his countrymen rendered him at the crisis in his fortunes. After ascending the throne, he sent a commission into Wales to enquire into and publish his Welsh descent. He wished to proclaim to the world that he was descended from the Welsh princely line.

Henry's flimsy bodyguard of under 50 men, although surprised by the onslaught of over 1,000 or more knights, were able effectively to protect him. It is highly probable that Henry's bodyguard was mainly composed of his fellow countrymen, Welsh noblemen from Dyfed and Gwynedd and their personal followers.

Henry's own fighting ability was under no doubt; he fought like a tiger. There can be little doubt that the support that Henry received from Wales was a major factor in his winning the throne and that Henry appreciated this. On his coinage it was the dragon of Wales which shared with the Beaufort greyhound the privilege of supporting his crown.

Many of his bodyguard from Wales were made members of the Yeomen of the Guard, which is probably the oldest body of troops in Britain today. Even today there is still a smattering of Welshmen in that Guard. Sir Rhys ap Thomas liked to think that his family were descended from the Lord Rhys but there is little evidence for this. Sir Rhys was knighted on the battlefield and given great power in Wales. His views were often sought by Henry on matters political, military and judicial.

Sir Rhys's military talents were enlisted by the King on several occasions in the first dozen years of the reign, against both enemies at home and abroad. When Sir Thomas Vaughan of Tretower raised the standard of revolt at Brecon, Hay and Tretower, Sir Rhys ap Thomas with a substantial force of 140 men defended Brecon Castle for 7 weeks. He helped put down Lambert Simnel's rebellion in 1487, and when war with France became unavoidable, Sir Rhys with a retinue of 590 Welshmen assembled at Winchester. Also, he was crucial in the Cornish men's rising in 1497. The King's trust in, and indeed affection for Sir Rhys scarcely dimmed as the years passed. The most public sign of the esteem was that, within 18 months of the rout of Warbeck's rebellious army, Sir Rhys was elevated as a Knight, nominated on St George's Day, 1499 to the Order of the Garter. With the accession of Henry VIII to the throne, Sir Rhys was still fighting, this time commanding a large retinue of almost 3,000 infantry and light cavalry.

Rhys received much reward for his part in the battles in France, including 500 marks from Henry himself. He returned to Wales still with great influence. His reputation was that of an immensely distinguished and influential Welsh Knight, widely admired for his chivalric style and military experience. Sir Rhys died in the summer of 1525 at the age of 76, and was buried in the Greyfriars Church in Carmarthen.

During his long life, Sir Rhys had formed a large circle of friends and servants, officials and councillors. His family had been a stout pillar of early Tudor rule. He was a great Welshman who made a huge contribution to Welsh culture with his support of the bards, and his loyalty to both Henry VII and Henry VIII was never questioned; He was one of the most powerful and eminent Welshmen of his day.

Henry Tudor and Wales. Glanmor Williams, University of Wales Press, 1985

Bosworth Field, A Welsh Retrospect. Emyr Wyn Jones, Modern Welsh Publications Ltd, 1984

Sir Rhys ap Thomas and his Family. Ralph A Griffiths, University of Wales Press, 2014

Sir Rhys ap Thomas. David Rees, Gomer Press, 1992

Queen Elizabeth I

THE GREAT WELSH WARRIOR QUEEN ELIZABETH I AND HER WELSH ADVISORS

Elizabeth was the only child of Henry VIII by his second wife Anne Boleyn. It was stated that the Williams's of Penpont, Brecon once bore the name of Bullen or Bollein and that Anne was an offshoot of that ancient stock.

It was said that Queen Elizabeth was very Welsh in character. A N Wilson says, 'On a market day in a Welsh town, you will pass by about 10 or 20 women with something of a look of Queen Elizabeth'. She was surrounded by a Tudor Tafia, according to Dr David Starkey.

As a young princess, she had entrusted her cofferer, Welshman Thomas Parry with some of her closest secrets and missions. Parry's daughter Blanche, the chief gentlewoman of the bedchamber, one of the Queens closet intimates and her apothecary was Welshman Hugh Morgan.

She was distrustful of those around her, economic of truth, thrifty even to stinginess if not at times intractable. There is an element of stereotyping here, but even with stereotyping there is often no smoke without fire.

Archbishop Dr Edwards of Wales said all these characteristics can be read in a face typically Welsh.

Her father, Henry VIII had done much to alleviate the restriction on liberties which had been forced on the Welsh after the Glyndwr revolt by his Act of Union which gave the Welsh representation in parliament.

There is some doubt as to whether Elizabeth spoke some Welsh but she was good at languages and Blanche Parry who became mistress of her bedchamber and was maid of honour may well have taught her some Welsh.

It is said that she encouraged the translation of the Bible into Welsh and that, in 1563, on the advice of Sir William Cecil she ordered by Act of Parliament that the four Welsh bishops and the Bishop of Hereford should undertake the translation into vernacular Welsh of the old and new testaments and also of the English prayer book under a heavy penalty for delay. There is no doubt that this helped to save the language.

Her chief counsellor was William Cecil who became Lord Burghley. Cecil was third in descent from an old Welsh family, the Seisyllts of Allt yr Ynys. They were descended from David Cecil who fought with Henry Tudor at Bosworth, and it is said that they were one of the few of the leading Welsh local families who avoided the massacre of the Welsh at Abergavenny Castle by the Normans.

Forty years of service was to prove that Elizabeth's judgement of her first minister was not at fault. Cecil was not only trustworthy, but he did not hesitate to tell the Queen when she was wrong or thought to be so.

She invariably took his advice.

Next in importance to Lord Burleigh was Sir William Herbert, a stalwart Welshman and first Earl of Pembroke of the second creation. He was a soldier, and one of the ablest.

It is a mystery to many of us how the original Herbert was William ap Thomas, and even in discussion with the Earl of Caernarvon quite recently, it is assumed that they changed their name because a French name was more fashionable than a Welsh one.

In the first year of her reign, Lord Williams of Thame was appointed president of the Council of Wales; he was related to Richard Williams, alias Cromwell. Elizabeth had once stayed in his house and was treated very kindly by him so, although he had been a supporter of her sister Mary, he was given this important appointment but unfortunately fell ill and died a few months later.

Another Welshman, Sir John Perrot, was made Lord Deputy of Ireland but he fell into disrepute with the Queen and was almost executed.

Sir John Price of Brecon took an active part in the union of Wales and England and was stated to have been the person who dictated the petition to Henry VIII, was knighted and died probably in 1572. He obviously had no influence in Elizabeth's reign but, from the author's point of view, showed that Brecon did have some influence with the Tudors.

We are assured that Sir Philip Sidney, who won immortal fame by his heroics at Zutphen, was of Welsh descent. He passed by the chance, despite being mortally wounded of receiving water in favour of another casualty and was a prebendary of Christ College, Brecon. He is said to have been of Welsh descent on his grandmother's side.

Lord Herbert of Cherbury, soldier, gallant, diplomatist, courtier, philosopher, historian, lover and mystic was a knight errant full of chivalrous adventure and a great favourite with the ladies; his famous autobiography was said to be one of the hundred best books. His great grandfather was steward under Henry VIII of the lordships and marches of north Wales, of east Wales and Cardiganshire.

Queen Elizabeth's navy consisted of only about 30 ships, the greatest of them being no bigger than the smallest ship in the Armada. One of the Welshmen who helped to augment the Elizabethan navy was Piers Griffith, who became a distinguished naval commander, marrying Margaret, daughter of Sir Thomas Mostyn and lies buried in Westminster Abbey.

Captain William Middleton, another naval commander, came to be the first with Captain Thomas Price to smoke tobacco in London; both of these men were poets.

Sir Robert Mansell of Glamorgan was another brave and skilful seaman and naval administrator of Elizabethan times.

Lord Burleigh's son, Sir Robert Cecil, took over from his father as chief minister and was quite as sharp as his father. Blanche Parry of Breconshire, who was related to the Herberts and owned Llangorse Lake, was a great confidant of the Queen in her bedchamber. Sir Thomas Parry, one of her relations, was the Queen's accountant.

Lastly, Dr John Dee who was a cousin of Blanche Parry and became close to the Queen was a necromancer and considered a magician and the Queen consulted him on astrology and it is said that once the Queen said to him after founding Virginia, *'What shall we call this new empire, John?'* And he said, *'Ma'am, you and I are the old Brits; we shall call it the British Empire, not the English Empire.'*

Dee's conversations with spirits fill a large folio volume, written evidently with the utmost sincerity. He was a lover of the Welsh language and came from a Welsh family.

He was an extraordinary man; not only did he develop the concept of the British Empire, he was into map reading and navigation. He translated Euclid and had the greatest library in England. He owned the Voynich manuscript, a cipher which hasn't been broken to this day; he founded the Rosicrucian order as an antidote to the Jesuits; he advised Queen Elizabeth on matters celestial and he spied for her in Europe and used the code name 007.

Henry VIII never set foot in Wales during his reign, but although the Act of Union disenfranchised many of the Welsh speakers in the assize, it did enfranchise many Welshmen who had been restricted in their rights before. Elizabeth obviously had a rapport with her Welsh counsellors which made them very much a 'Tafia' during her reign.

She was a great Warrior Queen, probably one of Britain's greatest monarchs, who initiated The British Empire.

The Elizabethans. A N Wilson, Hutchinson London, 2011

Elizabeth. David Starkey, Vintage, 2001

The Welsh Elizabethans. Frederick J Harries, Glamorgan County times, Pontypridd, 1924

Oliver Cromwell

OLIVER CROMWELL NÉ WILLIAMS
AND THE WELSH REGICIDES

Although Oliver Cromwell only visited Wales twice, once to suppress several thousand of its rebellious inhabitants and once on route to Ireland, he was by descent a Welshman.

Much was made under the protectorate from a heraldic point of view, of Cromwell's descent from the princes of Powys. Cromwell's forebears were a very typical minor Welsh gentry family.

They were said to be a brewing family from Glamorgan, and his great great grandfather was Morgan Williams, who emigrated to England. A change of surname was made to Cromwell, partly to curry favour with the infamous maternal uncle, Thomas Cromwell.

Henry VIII disapproved of the aps and naps which made those of Welsh descent hard to identify in English judicial procedure, and insisted on family names of a more substantial kind.

Oliver's grandfather Henry Cromwell had been dubbed a knight by Queen Elizabeth I in 1563. In the magnificent house at Hinchinbroke, a family seat of much splendour, the stained glass windows did not fail to commemorate the family's Welsh origins. In fact, when he was Lord Protector, Oliver was said to sign papers, 'Cromwell né Williams.'

In the English Civil War, he became one of the Parliamentarians' greatest commanders. He was particularly good at commanding cavalry, and, time and again, battles were won when Cromwell having defeated the opposite Royalist wing of cavalry brought his troops round in good order to attack the Royalist centre, whereas Prince Rupert would engage in ferocious charges, often defeating the opposite wing but his troops did not have the discipline to prevent rout, rape and pillage which took their minds off the battle.

Cromwell again was highly instrumental in forming the New Model Army and imposing on it a professional discipline. The author once said to the First Minister of Wales that Elizabeth I (Tudor) put many of the Scottish settlers in Ireland, Oliver Cromwell's original name was Williams, and Lloyd George put the Black and Tans into Ireland and so could we have a public apology from the Welsh to the Irish?

The First Minister said his wife was Irish and the author said that he'd better start in the bedroom then!

Cromwell's behaviour in Ireland was irreprehensible, and although there has been recent research which has suggested he did not give the orders for the massacre at Droghoda, as the commander in chief he was ultimately responsible.

He was a man of many contrasts, often tolerant towards for instance the Jews, and it was he that really established parliament as a major player in the constitution. When he died, he was interred in a vault in Westminster Abbey at the east end of Henry VII's chapel.

After the Restoration, his corpse was solemnly exhumed from the Abbey by a mason named John Lewis. The corpse was dragged through the streets of London from Holborn to Tyburn on open hurdles. At 10 o'clock, after the dragging through the city, the body was hung up in full gaze of the public; at 4 o'clock it was taken down and the common hangman proceeded to hack off the head. The headless trunk was consigned into a deep pit dug beneath the gallows of Tyburn, and the head was taken down to Westminster and 5 days later stuck on a pole of oak where it mouldered in a state of decomposition until 1684.

The story goes that it was blown down in a monster gale towards the end of the reign of James II, falling at the feet of one of the sentinels, the skull was picked up by the man who hid it under his cloak. It eventually passed into the hands of a dissolute and drunk actor called Samuel Russell and was later acquired by James Cox, proprietor of a museum. He in turn sold it to speculators who exhibited it at the time of the French Revolution and it eventually came into the hands of Canon Wilkinson who left it to Cromwell's old college Cambridge Sidney Sussex.

With regard to the Welsh Regicides, the main one of note was John Jones from Llanbedr in Merioneth. Jones, although he opposed the establishment of Cromwell's Protectorate, in December 1653 served as a commissioner for the militia in Wales during the rule of the major generals.

After Cromwell's death, he became commander in chief in the army in Ireland, and made no attempt to escape at the Restoration. He was arrested as a regicide in June, 1660 having signed the death warrant of Charles I. He was hanged, drawn and quartered on 17th October 1660, conducting himself bravely at his execution.

It is interesting that in Breconshire, there was a Colonel Jenkin Jones who had been converted by that great apostle of the Puritans in Breconshire Vavsor Powell. He raised a troop of horse amounting to six score and with their assistance kept the King's friends in Breconshire in complete subjection. There is no evidence he was executed but lost his wealth.

The inhabitants of Brecon were said to have destroyed the walls of the town to prevent the town's destruction by either side in the Civil War. Colonel Jenkin Jones was based at Llandetty.

Another Welshman, Thomas Wogan, was number 52 of the 59 signatories on the death warrant of the king. He was imprisoned after the Restoration but managed to escape from York Castle to the Netherlands before execution.

From the point of view of the author's local interest in Breconshire, one of the primary Parliamentary officers was Col Jenkin Jones from Llandetty. He is said to have matriculated from Jesus College Oxford in 1639 and although a preponderance of the gentry of Breconshire drew sword for the King, he was unswervingly loyal to Parliament. He raised, equipped and maintained at his own expense a troop of 120 horse from his relations, dependents and tenants.

He was one of the approvers 'Godly and painful men of approved conversation to preach the Gospel in Welsh'.

As an itinerant preacher, he received payment from the government. When Charles II was brought back as king, the event was so hateful to Jenkin Jones that he mounted his horse and riding through the churchyard in Llandetty discharged his pistol at the priest's door, exclaiming with great bitterness, 'Ah, the old whore of Babylon thou'lt have it all thy own way now'.

With the return of the king, his estates were confiscated and he was incarcerated in Carmarthen Gaol. He eventually disappeared to prison again.

Cromwell our Chief of Men. Lady Antonia Fraser, Orion, 1999

Stuart Wales, W S K Thomas. Gomer Press, 1988

Oliver Cromwell. John Buchan, Hodder & Stoughton, 1944

The Regicides and the Execution of Charles I, Jason Dr Peacey, AIAA, 2001

The Trial of Charles I, C V Wedgwood, The Fontana Library, 1964

Henry Morgan

CAPTAIN SIR HENRY MORGAN THE PIRATE

The great Welsh 'buccaneer' Henry Morgan acquired a very lurid reputation through the publication of *The Buccaneers of America* by A.O. (Alexander Oliver, though early English translations call him John) Exquemelin, a Dutch sailor who was with him at the rape of Panamá. Exquemelin's book was published in English in 1684.

Morgan was upset by it and eventually was awarded damages, apparently the first case of money being awarded for a literary libel. But it seems that what upset him most was not the accounts of torture and pillage, distressing as these are, but the account Exquemelin gives of his origins. Exquemelin claimed that he had run way from home and joined a ship going to Barbados as an indentured servant. Other versions said he had been kidnapped in Bristol, or that he had been sold by his parents.

As a result of Morgan's challenge, one of the English publishers of Exquemelin's book added in explanation:

'John Exquemelin hath mistaken the origin of Sir Henry Morgan, for he was a Gentleman's Son of good Quality, in the County of Monmouth, and was never a Servant unto anybody in his life, unless unto his Majesty, the late King of England.'

Most historians now think he was the eldest son of the Robert Morgan of Llanrhymney, near Cardiff, a yeoman farmer related to the Morgans of Tredegar, in which case he would have been quite well connected. One of his uncles would have been Edward Morgan, who was to become Deputy Governor of Jamaica. Henry married his uncle's daughter, his cousin, Mary Elizabeth.

The circumstances of Morgan's arrival in Jamaica are also debated. The idea most commonly accepted is that he arrived with the army sent by Oliver Cromwell in pursuit of what was called the 'Western Design', an attempt to strengthen the English position in the West Indies, indeed perhaps to prepare the way for a full English takeover of Spanish possessions in the area. The plan was to begin with the seizure of the Spanish island of Hispaniola (present day Haiti and Santo Domingo).

The attempt on Hispaniola in April 1655 was, in the event, a disaster. The invasion turned into a humiliating rout, with perhaps six hundred soldiers killed at the hands of a couple of hundred Spanish, many of them black slaves.

The English then turned their attention to Jamaica. It was taken with ease, but the occupation quickly fell into chaos. The American, Major Robert Sedgwick who arrived soon afterward wrote back to London, ' Should I give you a character of the dispositions and qualifications of our army in general (some few particulars excepted), I profess my heart would grieve to write, as it doth to think of them. I believe they are not to be paralleled in the whole world; a people so lazy and idle, as it cannot enter into the heart of any Englishman that such blood should run in the veins of any born in England - so unworthy, slothful, and basely secure; and have, out of a strange kind of spirit, desired rather die than live ...'

This helps to explain the importance of the privateers and buccaneers in the early history of Jamaica.

Buccaneering methods were used from the start by Vice-Admiral Goodson, who had remained behind with twelve ships after the departure of the English fleet. In October 1655 he launched a raid on the town of Santa Marta de la Victoria, near Cartagena on the mainland in what is now Colombia - it was then part of the Audiencia of Santa Fe. The population fled with their possessions. Goodson pursued them for twelve miles, then plundered and burnt their houses. Some weeks later, his lieutenant, Captain Nuberry, returned and found that some of the people had begun to rebuild, so he burnt them a second time.

The Santa Marta attack was followed by a very similar raid in April 1656 on Rio de la Hacha. Thereafter, through 1657 and 1658, Goodson attempted to seize the Spanish treasure fleet but eventually it slipped through his hands and, apparently, in spite, the English then destroyed the town of Tolú, also in Santa Fe and, yet again, Santa Marta, destroying everything for miles around.

But the real triumph came in 1659, when Captain Christopher Myngs arrived with what the historian Clarence Haring calls 'the richest prize that ever entered Jamaica.' They had attacked the towns of Cumana, Puerto Cabello and Coro, all on the coast of Venezuela. At Coro they followed the fleeing inhabitants into the woods where they found twenty two chests of treasure, each containing 400 lbs of silver, intended for the King of Spain. Together with plates, jewels and cocoa, the whole came to something between £20,000 and £30,000, a huge sum at the time.

With the restoration of the monarchy in England in 1660 it looked for a moment as if this policy of brigandage might have to change. A new governor, Lord Windsor, arrived with instructions 'to endeavour to obtain and preserve a good correspondence and free commerce with the plantations belonging to the King of Spain.' To this end, however, he was empowered to use force. He arrived accompanied by Christopher Myngs, with a forty six gun frigate, *The Centurion*. The following month Myngs sailed out with some 1,300 men and eleven ships to raid the nearest Spanish port, Santiago, after Havana the most important port in Cuba. As one historian comments: 'the soldiery, poor and destitute of the necessary means of settling, joyfully embraced the opportunity of pillage.' The fortress was razed to the ground and Myngs returned to a hero's welcome.

The following January, 1663, Myngs set out again, this time to San Francisco de Campeche, in the Gulf of Mexico, near Yucatan. He was badly wounded during this raid and the command was briefly taken by the buccaneer, Edward Mansfield, or Mansveldt. As a result of his wounds Myngs returned to England in July with *The Centurion*. He would be active in the Anglo-Dutch war in 1664, promoted to Vice-Admiral and knighted for his involvement in the battle of Lowestoft in June 1665.

In January 1664, Thomas Modyford, a well-known planter in Barbados was appointed as governor of

Jamaica. As England was involved in a war with the Dutch, an expedition was organised with a very ambitious programme of capturing the Dutch properties of St Eustatia, Saba and Curaçao and then, on the return journey, the French stations at Tortuga and Hispaniola. It was led by Modyford's deputy, Col Edward Morgan. They took St Eustatia and Saba with embarrassing ease - the Dutch put up no resistance - but Morgan, an old man, died in the heat. This expedition of privateers led by an army officer with targets specified by the council was on the same pattern as the exploits of Captain Myngs but it hardly had Myngs's charismatic leadership. It broke up in disputes over the division of the spoil (some 900 Negroes with livestock and cotton) and returned to Jamaica with a clear sense of failure.

It was at this point, on 20th August 1665, that a group of privateers, led by a Captain Fackman or Jackman, arrived in Jamaica. Fackman was accompanied by a Captain Morris and a Captain Morgan and it is generally assumed that these were the Welshmen, John Morris and Henry Morgan.

They arrived with a tale of derring-do starting with an ascent up the river Tabasco in the Campeche province guided by Indians to the (largely Indian populated) town of Villa de Moos - Villahermosa - which they took and plundered. On their return to the mouth of the Tabasco they found that their ships had been seized by the Spanish. With 100 men they fought off 300 Spanish but failed to regain the ships. Using two barques and four canoes they crossed the Gulf of Honduras then traversed the Mosquito coast 'like a devouring flame, consuming all in their path', to quote one admiring account, until they reached Monkey Bay. They ascended the San Juan River in canoes for one hundred miles to Lake Nicaragua and then, accompanied by 1,000 Indians, they took and plundered the city of Granada.

It was all stirring stuff and arrived at a quite propitious moment. Modyford had abandoned the policy of trying to organise the privateers under the command of army officers and turned instead for leaders to the buccaneers themselves. A reunion was held at Bluefields Bay in Jamaica which elected Edward Mansfield as their head for an expedition supposedly against the Dutch at Curaçao. But it was really rather fanciful to expect that this pirate band, led by a Dutchman, would be interested in attacking the Dutch when there were so many very much easier Spanish targets to attack.

The expedition, predictably, never came anywhere near Curaçao. It started by raiding Santo Spirito in Cuba then went on to Boca del Toro, on the borderline between Panamá and Costa Rica. Then they launched another raid on Granada, the victim of Fackman's exploits the previous year, and harried Costa Rica, 'burning plantations, breaking the images in the churches, hamstringing cows and mules, cutting down the fruit trees and in general destroying everything they found', to quote Haring.

On his way back, Mansfield, probably trying to think of something that could be construed as a service to the King of England, attacked Santa Catalina, a small island strategically positioned in the middle of the ocean off the Nicaraguan (or 'Mosquito') coast. This had been 'Providence Island', originally occupied by the English Providence Island Company, which had been active in persuading Cromwell to adopt the Western Design. It could be represented as a matter of reclaiming British territory and after Mansfield returned to Jamaica in June 1666, Modyford sent an army officer, Major Samuel Smith, to strengthen it while in England Modyford's brother, Sir James Modyford, was appointed governor. But in August, in a rare display of energy, the Spanish took it back again. The treatment of the prisoners they took was to provide some colour of justification for the subsequent depredations of Henry Morgan.

Morgan may have participated with Mansfield in the seizure of Providence. Exquemelin gives him a leading role but he also states, inaccurately, that Modyford did not support the venture. Exquemelin only arrived in the region in 1666 and only met up with Morgan a couple of years later so his account is based on hearsay.

The really salient characteristic of Morgan's career up to 1668, is its obscurity - an obscurity that persists through the latter part of 1666, from the time of Mansfield's return in June, assuming Morgan had been part of his operation, through the whole of 1667, to early in 1668. It was not a period in which nothing was happening. Early in 1666, the French entered into alliance with the Dutch and there was intense fighting between French and English, with some Dutch involvement, through the Antilles. But during this period, when the English interest in the West Indies really was under attack from formidable enemies, Henry Morgan seems to have been inactive. It may have been then that he married Edward Morgan's recently orphaned daughter, Mary Elizabeth, and began his alternative career as a planter.

Modyford was now clearly committed to the view that the wellbeing of Jamaica required a permanent state of war. From this perspective the peace with Spain that was concluded in Madrid in May 1667 was bad news. It was publicly announced in Jamaica and at about the same time Modyford gave a commission to Henry Morgan - the moment when he first appears unequivocally as a leading figure on the stage - 'to draw together the English privateers and take prisoners of the Spanish nation, whereby he might inform of [sic] the intention of that enemy to invade Jamaica.'

Morgan sailed off early in 1668. He sailed to Cuba, demanded provisions and used the predictable refusal as an excuse to go inland, wasting and pillaging everywhere he went. He went to Puerto de Principe where, naturally he learned that the Spanish were indeed planning an invasion of Jamaica and of course that musters were being summoned at towns on the mainland which meant he would have to go there. So far so banal. It was his choice of target that distinguished him from the ordinary run of buccaneers. He chose to go to Portobello.

Portobello was a town on the coast of Panamá which derived its importance from the great treasure fleets that sailed from America to Spain. The source of the treasure was the mines on the Pacific side, the west coast, of the country.

The isthmus of Panamá was the shortest route from the west to the east. The produce of the mines was brought to Panamá on the west coast then transported to Portobello on the east coast to be loaded onto the ships to face the long dangerous journey to Europe. But these sailings of the treasure fleet had become more and more infrequent. They were now held only once every two years.

At that moment Panamá and Portobello were like something out of a fairy tale with a vast temporary population surrounded by the signs of unimaginable wealth. Otherwise they were both rather depressing places situated in an area notorious for disease. Peter Earle describes Portobello as 'a stinking, half-empty fever hole' which, however, because of its importance at the times of the fleet, was, or at least was reputed to be, well fortified.

Exquemelin gives a very dramatic account of the actual seizure of Portobello but it should probably be read in the light of Peter Earle's version based on research in the Spanish archives. Exquemelin says Morgan put soldiers and officers into a single room then blew it up with gunpowder, but this does not appear in Earle's account. Exquemelin has the governor in one of the two forts overlooking the port putting up a desperate fight until eventually Morgan used religious men and women to set the siege ladders, forcing the defenders to fire on them - the Spanish account has a little group of citizens including friars and nuns being used as human shields while the English approached the main door with axes and fire. The Spanish accounts do not repeat Exquemelin's accounts of torture but Earle does not think that is a reason for disbelieving them.

Morgan threatened to torch the city unless a ransom was paid. He initially demanded 350,000 pesos in silver but eventually settled for 100,000. It was this, not what he found in Portobello, that enabled him to count the expedition a financial success. He was in Portobello for fifteen days 'in which space of time', Exquemelin says, 'they had lost many of their men, both by the unhealthiness of the country and the extravagant debauch they had committed.' They brought the fever back with them to Jamaica and Modyford's wife, among others, died of it.

The rape of Portobello was, however, immensely popular among a British public demoralised by ten years of fire, plague and defeat at the hands of the Dutch, and uneasy at the peace with Spain, the hereditary enemy, at the change of mood since the more glorious days of the Commonwealth and suspicious of the possibility of papist influence in court. It looked like a glorious English victory and the court was not above taking advantage of it. They assumed a high tone, insisting that the peace treaty did not cover the West Indies where the Spanish refused to recognise English possessions and had only recently invaded Providence Island and had the clear intention, as proved by the depositions obtained by Morgan, to invade Jamaica.

In October 1668, Morgan was off again to the Isla Vaca, off the coast of Hispaniola, to gather a new band of privateers for a further adventure which, if it was to be more spectacular than Portobello, had to be either Panamá or Cartagena, capital of the Audiencia of Santa Fe. These were the towns that the audience back in England would have heard of. His possibilities were enhanced enormously when, shortly afterwards, he was joined by a thirty-four gun frigate, the *Oxford*, a gift from the Lord High Admiral, the Duke of York, to Modyford.

With such means at their disposal, Morgan and his cronies fixed on Cartagena as their target but as they were celebrating the coming adventure, an accidental spark, apparently, in the powder room, blew the ship up. Morgan himself had been feasting on the deck. All those on the opposite side of the table from him were killed. Those on his side of the table were thrown into the sea and had to be fished out. This naturally rather dampened the spirits of the assembly Morgan had brought together and the

98

group broke up. Morgan was left with a small flotilla of undecked ships reduced to eight, with five hundred men, about half the original number.

Under these circumstances, the best he could do was to repeat the exploit performed two years earlier by the French privateer, Jean-David Nau, 'L'Ollonais', and attack Maracaibo in the Gulf of Venezuela. Maracaibo was situated in a huge salt water lake which was connected to the Gulf by a narrow pass. Morgan found that, since the visit of L'Ollonais, a fort had been built at the pass. By good fortune, however, it was seriously undermanned, with only eight men and a castellan who, after a brief spirited defence, lost their nerve and crept away. Exquemelin tells us they left a long slow fuse running to the powder magazine but Morgan spotted it and stamped it out in the nick of time.

Morgan made a good haul of slaves, jewels, silk, pieces of eight and prisoners to be ransomed but it was still just an ordinary pirate raid without the element of glory that seems to have been so important to him. That, however, was about to change.

By the mid-1660s privateering attacks on the Spanish colonies were so widespread that the authorities in Spain had finally sent a small fleet of five well-armed, rapid ships to deal with it. It sailed in July 1667 and was actually in Havana at the very moment when Morgan was raiding Puerto de Principe and sailing to Portobello. In July 1668, after the raid on Portobello, orders were received recalling two of the ships. The Vice-Admiral of the three ships that were left, Don Alonzo de Campas, had learned of the intended raid on Cartagena and finally discovered that Morgan's ships were bottled up in what was more or less the perfect trap of Lake Maracaibo. All he had to do was to invest the bottle neck leading to the Gulf and wait for them to come out.

It was here that Morgan, or at least Morgan's team, revealed something resembling genius. What they did was to prepare a 'fire ship' - a ship primed to explode. But it was decked out as a flagship. It was equipped with logs disguised as canons and as men. It came on ahead looking as if it was Morgan's own ship, daringly headed straight for De Campos's main ship, the *Magdalena*. Once the two ships were in contact the small team piloting the fire ship escaped and it blew up, taking the *Magdalena* with it. The second of the Spanish ships, the *San Luis*, seeing that the situation of the *Magdalena* was hopeless, was beached in an effort to gain the fort, while the third, the smallest, the *Nuestra Senora de Soledad*, got its sails in a muddle and was seized as a prize by the pirates. The victory over the 'Armada de Barlovento' was complete.

That still left the port, which still commanded the bottleneck and now had a garrison to man its guns. Morgan attempted to storm it but was repeatedly repulsed, losing many of his men. Eventually he got out through an old but spectacularly successful ruse. In sight of the fort, he landed successive boatloads of buccaneers in a nearby mangrove swamp. He was obviously preparing a land assault.

As a result, De Campos moved his guns so that they were facing landward. But in fact the buccaneers landed in the swamp had returned to their ships concealed in the apparently empty canoes that had brought them out. In the night, the ships slipped their anchor and drifted past the fort. They were seen but by the time the guns had been brought back again, they were through and safe.

The privateers sailed back in triumph, arriving in Port Royal, on the 27th May, 1669, headed by Morgan's new flagship, *Nuestra Senora de Soledad*. An expedition which had started in disaster had ended in glory with the destruction of the only defensive sea force the Spanish had in the area.

In the meantime, in reaction to the humiliation at Portobello, the Queen Regent in Spain had sent instructions that the Spanish authorities could do to the English what the English authorities had been doing to the Spanish. Private individuals could 'proceed against the English in the Indies with every sort of hostility ...'

On the receipt of this letter, the governor of Cartagena, in October 1699, publicly announced war with Jamaica and a number of incidents occurred which indicated to the Jamaicans that the Spanish were adopting a more aggressive approach. These climaxed in the activities of the Portuguese corsair, Manoel Rivero Pardal who made a couple of landings in the sparsely populated parts of Jamaica and burned some houses. This was a flea bite but the Jamaicans, so used to operating with impunity, did not know what it might mean for the future.

As a result of all this, Morgan was given a commission to assemble a force 'and if necessary attack any place inland that he suspected was being used for war.' Among those who joined him was John Morris, fresh from the triumph of having killed Pardal and seized his ship. Another ship that had worked with Pardal, *La Gallardina*, was also seized. The Spanish captain of *La Gallardina* was hanged by Morgan for declining to give evidence that an invasion was being prepared at Cartagena and Panamá, but two of the crew duly agreed. As Morgan's surgeon, Richard Browne, put it: 'Some through torments, confesse what wee please. Other more ingenious and stoute will not be drawne to speake or subscribe what they know not, who are then cutt in pieces, shott or hanged.'

Morgan now had the pretext he needed for what was to be the great achievement of his life, the rape of Panamá, and he had the largest assembly of privateers yet seen in the West Indies. Morgan planned to attack Panamá along the river Chagre, which was protected by a fort, San Lorenzo. He sent three ships ahead under the command of Lt Col Joseph Bradley, to reduce the fort before the main body of the privateers would follow.

At Lake Maracaibo we have seen that Morgan initially encountered a well-built fort manned by a pathetically small garrison. At San Lorenzo, Bradley encountered a badly built fort manned by a garrison that was both strong - equal in numbers to Bradley's force - and well led. But the fort was built of wood and straw, and the privateers succeeded, probably to their own amazement, in setting it alight. Bradley died as a result of the attack together with over a hundred of his men. Morgan arrived some days later in his flagship, *The Satisfaction*, which, together with the four ships following, sailed straight on to a reef and broke up. Peter Earle wonders if the seamanship of the buccaneers was always all it was cracked up to be.

What follows - the march to Panamá on the west side of the isthmus, was a monument to dogged determination and courage in facing the unknown. The trek across the isthmus was hellish. Morgan had expected the jungle to be full of game and had wanted his men to travel light so, once the boats had been abandoned, they were not carrying food. In fact the jungle yielded nothing they could recognise as being edible and the Spaniards were retreating before them destroying any possible source of provisions as they went. After four days without food, the pirate army was a disorganised rabble which could probably have been routed easily. But, alas for the Spanish, no sooner did they leave the jungle than they encountered a plain full of cattle.

Panamá lay before them - an open city without fortifications. The 'army' standing between the pirates and Panamá, though numerous, was made up of the more courageous citizens together with a large number of black slaves and Indians. Now that the pirates were fed and rested this was all simply feeble, the more so because the Spanish had neglected to defend a small hill on their right flank. Once the English had seized that, the victory was won.

It was followed by a scene from hell as the citizenry, crazed with fear, set fire to the town. Historians have questioned if this was the work of the English or the Spanish but the Spanish accounts leave no room for doubt. It was not at all in the interests of the English to find themselves presiding over a heap of charred timber in the middle of a disease-ridden swamp. There was the usual job to be done rounding up the citizens and torturing them to get hold of their valuables, but the biggest prizes had disappeared on three ships which had been loaded and got away before the city fell.

On 24th February, after an occupation that had lasted four weeks, they left. Inevitably, Morgan's army broke up. Some were shipwrecked on the central American coast.

Long's *History of Jamaica* tells us that 'In 1671, when the fleet commanded by Sir Henry Morgan returned from that coast, his crews brought with them the malignant fever of Portobello, and the greater part of them died of it; the contagion spread to those on shore where it produced a terrible mortality.' From the point of view of Morgan's political intentions - if we can guess what they were - we may wonder if the venture really succeeded. Although piracy in the region was to have a great future and Jamaica remained at the centre of it, Panamá marked the end of the policy of piracy sponsored as a matter of government policy.

A decision to replace Sir Thomas Modyford had already been made in December 1670, before the news of the rape of Panamá had arrived. His successor was Thomas Lynch, knighted for the occasion. Lynch was himself a Jamaica planter. He had left Jamaica in 1665, after Modyford had removed him from the council and from his office of chief justice, probably about the time Modyford was committing himself to a policy of encouraging the privateers.

He now returned with clear instructions to suppress privateering and encourage agriculture. He also had the delicate task of arresting Modyford and Morgan, the two most popular men on the island, whose policies had brought in so much easily obtained wealth. Modyford was kept for some months imprisoned on a ship before being sent to London where he was put in the Tower of London.

He was still there in 1674 though he was back in Jamaica by 1676. Morgan was not arrested until 1672, perhaps because he was ill, presumably with the fever he had brought back with him from Panamá. When he did go to London, however, he was 'lionised', everyone wanting to bask in the glory of the conqueror of Panamá and enjoy the excitement of associating with such a dashing rogue.

His main problem was that being lionised in such circles was an expensive business and he was quickly running through his means but he was making connections which would be useful to him, including two future governors of Jamaica - the Earl of Carlisle and the Duke of Albemarle, son of General Monck, the Cromwellian leader who had been largely responsible for the restoration of Charles II.

Morgan was tried in 1673, defending himself on the absurd grounds that his attack on Panamá had been a war to end war, necessary to prevent a Spanish aggression. Soon after being acquitted he was knighted and appointed to return to Jamaica as lieutenant-governor together with Carlisle as governor.

In the event, however, Carlisle was unable to go and in 1675, Morgan and Carlisle's replacement, John Vaughan, departed in two separate ships. Morgan's ship, to Vaughan's annoyance, raced ahead. It was blown on to the Isla Vaca, losing much of its stores, but Morgan still reached Jamaica before Vaughan. It is not clear why Morgan was so anxious to arrive first. The loss of the stores - which included a great deal of military equipment - on the island that had been and still was the great meeting place of the privateers aroused feelings of suspicion.

Vaughan continued Lynch's policy of trying to suppress the privateers but soon found that he had a deadly enemy in Morgan. The two men were temperamentally unsuited to each other, despite their common Welsh origins. Vaughan was a highly cultured member of the aristocracy. He was Member of Parliament for the borough of Camarthen and the Vaughan estates were counted as among the largest in Wales. Eventually, however, worn down by the confrontation with Morgan and with the island's assembly, he left in March 1678. Carlisle arrived in July and, in the interim, Morgan ruled as lieutenant-governor.

Carlisle had come to Jamaica with instructions to introduce a new form of government, similar to the Irish 'Poyning's Law' which concentrated legislative power in the hands of the government in England. The result was a ferocious contest with the assembly which may have been a continuation of earlier disputes with Vaughan except that Morgan was now aligned with Carlisle and was passing himself off as a Tory and a King's man.

In May 1680, Carlisle left to argue his case in London. Morgan was left in charge and seemed full of drive and energy. He had two new forts built - Fort Rupert and Fort Carlisle, and strengthened the already existing Fort James. He may have been inspired by a new aggressiveness among the Spaniards and by an edict from the King of France forbidding all privateering against the Spanish and withdrawing all existing commissions. The last thing Jamaica wanted was an alliance between France and Spain.

In London, the new constitutional arrangement was withdrawn and Lynch replaced Carlisle as governor. He seems to have returned with a determination to root out Morgan and his friends once and for all. He died in 1684 but the exclusion of the Morgan faction continued under his friend and close colleague, Hender Molesworth.

Morgan seems to have fallen into ever greater depths of alcoholism. He did, however, have one last moment of recognition when his old drinking companion from his days in London, Christopher Monck, second Duke of Albemarle, was appointed governor in November 1687. Albemarle had asked permission from the King to reappoint Morgan to the Council but he only received it in July 1688. Morgan died in August, at the age of fifty three. Albemarle himself died a couple of months later, of jaundice and dropsy.

They died on the eve of the 'Glorious Revolution', which brought the Dutch William of Orange to the throne of England. The result really did turn the world of Henry Morgan upside down. For the next twenty years, England would be an ally of Holland and Spain against France. Instead of the straw man enemy, Spain, Jamaica found itself at war with France. In these circumstances, the Jamaican planters were to have some small taste of the medicine Morgan and his predecessors had been giving the Spanish in America, relentlessly and with an amazing conviction of their own righteousness for the previous thirty years.

Admiral Sir Henry Morgan - The greatest buccaneer of them all. Terry Breverton, Glyndwr Publishing, 2005

*Rev George Wilson Bridges.*The Annals of Jamaica , vol i, London, John Murry, 1828

The Sack of Panama - Captain Morgan and the Battle for the Caribbean. Peter Earle: New York, Thomas Dunne Books, 2007 (first published in 1981)

The Pirate Wars. London, Methuen, 2004

The History, Civil and Commercial of the British Colonies in the West Indies. Bryan Edwards, Dublin, Luke White, 1793

The Buccaneers of America. Alexander O. Exquemelin, translated from the Dutch by Alexis Brown, New York, Dover Publications, 2000

The Buccaneers in the West Indies in the Seventeenth Century. C.H.Haring, London, Methuen and Co, 1910

Interesting Tracts relating to the Island of Jamaica. Consisting of curious state papers, councils of war, letters, petitions, narratives ..., St Iago de la Vega, 1800

General Henry Lloyd

GENERAL HENRY LLOYD

Few individuals could claim to have inspired both Gilbert and Sullivan and two of the greatest American generals of their time, but Humphrey Evans Lloyd went further, being well known to the three great Enlightenment despots of eighteenth century Europe and countless other European sovereigns.

From a curiously vague educational background, Lloyd's erratic career saw him ultimately become a favourite of Empress Catherine the Great of Russia, who not only commissioned him into her army as a Major General, but asked him to plan an invasion of China!

The Holy Roman Emperor Joseph II of Austria and Frederick the Great of Prussia were also on speaking terms. Yet, on his death, reactionary Catholics at Huy, near Liege, desecrated his body because of his radical political views.

They were not alone: Napoleon Bonaparte furiously scribbled denunciations of Lloyd's military theories, while the renowned military intellectual, von Clausewitz, was equally critical of his ideas. Yet he was later read by the likes of Generals George Washington and George Patton. Lloyd is even alluded to as the inspiration for Gilbert & Sullivan's wonderful patter song, "I am the Very Model of the Modern Major General". Whether true or false, the lyrics certainly describe General Lloyd 'to a T', while (led by Patrick Speelman) new books and articles about him are being published increasingly across the world. Yet this giant remains mostly invisible in his own country.

However, unearthing Lloyd's roots is still proving a bit of a problem: even his published birth dates vary by eight years! Supposedly, he descended from the Llwyd family of Cwm-bychan, Meirionydd, they of Ffarwel Dai Llwyd fame. Yet his own son, Hannibal, (what else?) says he was born at Wrecsam, a son of the Reverend John Lloyd. But then, in his own handwriting, he signed on at Jesus College, Oxford as the son of Ambrose Lloyd of Rhuthun, first classing himself as a 'servitor' (the lowest class of student), before crossing that out in favour of being a plebeian.

Although Lloyd could afford his board and lodging, his college attendance was not the best, and he failed to graduate. However, he made a valuable contact who was to prove a major influence on his thinking. The Jesus College principal at the time was the eminent Sir Watkin Williams Wynn, 3rd Baroner, known as the 'Prince of Wales' due to his political power both in Wales and Westminster. Sir Watkin was a leading Jacobite, and whatever the wellspring of his political views, Henry Lloyd too opposed the Hanoverian succession.

In the wake of his Jesus College sojourn, Lloyd's career remains equally vague: after a bit of 'lawyering' somewhere near home (and an affair with a ballerina in Berlin) we know our hero ended up fighting with Louis XV at Pontenoy, after spells in Venice, Barcelona, Madrid and (possibly in the guise of a lay Jesuit teacher) Sint-Omars in Flanders.

It was under Louis XV that Lloyd gained his first military commission as a sub-ensign, after which he sailed for Scotland with Prince Charles Edward Stuart ('Bonnie Prince Charlie') in 1745 – a move which was to add yet another dimension to his increasingly colourful life. Unlike his fellow officers who perished in the massacre at Culloden, Captain Lloyd of the Regiment Royal-Ecossais was heading for Wales on a secret (but as yet unchronicled) mission to foment Jacobite rebellion in his homeland – only to be captured by the King's police.

Placed under house arrest in Jermyn St, London, Lloyd was lucky to escape punishment under the severe sedition and exclusion laws in force at the time, and on release (almost certainly through Jacobite influence) scarpered back to Louis XV's army. Now a major, Lloyd, literally, helped engineer the bloody siege of Bergen op Zoom.

Lloyd lived at a hinge-point in the history of Europe. The Enlightenment – science, rationality and efficiency – opened up civilian and military offices to the better qualified.   Heredity, money and court connections mattered less, provided a strong monarchy remained in place. But it needed driven individuals like Lloyd to seize the day, and character mattered. Lloyd became multi-lingual, adding Latin, French, German, Italian and Spanish to his Welsh and English.

His manuscripts exist in English, French, German and Italian, although nothing in Welsh has yet emerged. He was a polymath, yet substantially self-educated as far as we know. He wrote and published on military theory and practice, much aided by his cartographical skills and possibly even a Napoleonic coup d'œil.

He seems to have been personally fearless, never afraid of a scrap. From suffering a shoulder injury in a sea battle while sailing to Scotland, to commanding a Russian division in the successful siege of Silestia on the Danube during the 2nd Russo-Turkish war, Lloyd was never an armchair general.

Yet in Milan, Lloyd was recognised as a leading figure in the city's particular form of enlightenment: It was his theory of money (unknown in Wales until the work of H D Matthews) which proved an essential driver in making that city a 'republic of money'. When you see Armani, Campari, Ferrari and Pirelli, pause briefly to think of our Henry.

Paradoxically the greater part off Lloyd's life was spent as a paid British agent. His ambition was to make a career as a professional soldier, but when peace broke out – as it so often did – Lloyd (like Spike Milligan's Bluebottle) must have said, 'You gotta make a living somehow'.

It seems he first took Hanoverian coin in 1767, his benefactor being the famous Marquis of Granby, now of public houses fame. There is evidence of Lloyd's work for British Intelligence wherever he went and regardless of the Army in which he served: as a Captain in Austria, Colonel in Braunschweig, honorary Major General in Cologne. Unfortunately, he failed to get a military appointment with King Jose I of Portugal, and lost his Milanese friends because of it.

But perhaps this leap from Jacobite rebel to Hanoverian 'snitch' is not as great as it seems. Many of Lloyd's UK government associates were military and political progressives, often with old Jacobite connections.

114

His wife, Mary, did not hide her Stuart-supporting family roots. Lloyd strongly favoured John Wilkes MP, the 'Father of Civil Liberty'. His essay on the English Constitution (1770) argued against the abuse of power against Wilkes, whose nemesis, Nathan Carrington, had been Lloyd's personal jailer back in 1746.

There is emerging evidence that Lloyd's world-view and means of personal advancement were aided by pan-European Masonic connections. His Milanese collaborator, Pietro Verri, was reputedly a leading freemason, while London's Jerusalem lodge had a 'Henry Lloyd' listed as a member in 1769, along with the philosopher Edmund Burke and (possibly) John Wilkes. Lloyd's first biographer, the Marquis de Romance de Mesmon (who published in 1784, only one year after Lloyd's death) was a member of the Parisian lodge, Saint-Jean-d'Ecosse Contrat social.

However, Lloyd's enlightened attitudes in public affairs were counter-balanced by his personality. Throughout his life, friend and foe alike remarked on his hot temper. In Milan, he insulted an Abbot. On his way to observe the Russo-Ottoman war in 1774, Lloyd had a public row with a Brugge coachman. Perhaps the greatest manifestation of his 'y gwir yn erbyn y byd' attitude was his commentary on the Empress of all Russias, 'She is under great obligations to me; I am under none to her'. Little wonder Catherine felt disinclined to award him her Order of St George, or its substantial pension.

The whole world knows the incredible but fictitious tales of Baron von Münchhausen, a near contemporary of Lloyd who also fought the Ottomans. As Henry Lloyd re-emerges from the historical murk, perhaps his almost unbelievable life adventure will command more attention by his fellow-countrymen and modern mythmakers across the world. Even if it's only half-true, what a story is waiting to be fully discovered and re-told.

Article by Syd Morgan, Cambria Magazine

General Sir Thomas Picton

GENERAL SIR THOMAS PICTON, WELLINGTON'S WELSH GENERAL

The Duke of Wellington called him *'A rough, foul mouthed devil as ever lived'*. This was probably why he never recommended him to be elevated as a lord, as he did with other of his prominent generals. The incident that epitomised Wellington's feelings towards Picton was when they retreated behind the lines of Torres Fedras, Picton's base being behind a farmhouse on a distant hill.

Wellington instructed his ADC to check on Picton and his staff and make sure they weren't having a drunken orgy. When the ADC got up there and looked in through the kitchen window, Picton and his staff were making lemonade from the local lemons – what innocence!

Picton was the seventh of twelve children of Thomas Picton, a Pembrokeshire squire and his wife Cecil nee Powell. He was born in Haverfordwest on about 24th August 1758. We know little of his early life except that his father had an estate, so he was brought up in the country. In 1771, he obtained an ensign's commission in the 12th Regiment of Foot.

The regiment was stationed in Gibraltar where there was a mutiny amongst the men where Picton first came to notice by quelling it with great courage. After retirement from the army, at this stage, he lived on his father's estate for nearly twelve years, but then he went out to the West Indies in 1794 being acquainted with Sir John Vaughan who made him his aide de camp and he was promoted major in the 58th of Foot.

After the capture of Trinidad in 1797, Picton was made governor of the island, holding this post for the next five years. His governorship was marked by brutal suppression, and Picton made money from speculation in land and slaves, influenced by his mulatto mistress.

In December 1803, Picton was arrested by order of the Privy Council. He was accused of excessive cruelty, severity to slaves and execution of suspects out of hand.

On certainly one or two occasions he had ordered the removal of eyelids as a punishment. One of the tortures included picketing and consisted in principle of compelling the trussed up suspect to stand on one toe on a flat headed peg for one hour on many occasions within a span of a few days.

Another method of questioning he allowed was of a young mulatto, Louisa Calderon who was suspended from a pulley set in the roof of the torture cell trussed up so that only one of her legs could dangle freely. She was then lowered on to a sharpened spike set in the floor, her naked foot first until her entire bodyweight rested on the spike.

Although Picton was found guilty, there was later a retrial and the verdict was reversed. This did his career little harm and he was soon promoted Major General and in 1809 he was governor of Flushing in the Netherlands during the Walcheren expedition.

In 1810 at Wellington's request Picton was appointed to command a division in Spain. He was recommended by

General Miranda who thought him extremely clever but untrustworthy. Although we have Wellington's comment about him at the beginning of this essay, Wellington went on to say, *'He always behaved extremely well, no man could do better in different services I assigned him'*.

After the winter in Torres Fedras he added to his increasing reputation and to that of his division the Fighting 3rd at the Battle of Fuentes de Onoro. He was made Lieutenant General and did brilliantly when the division retired in an orderly way under severe pressure from the French cavalry at El Bodon. In 1812 at Badajoz, he displayed huge courage in the attack on the fortress and was himself wounded.

At Vittoria, again he showed remarkable leadership. On 24th June, 1814 he received for the seventh time the thanks of the House of Commons for his great services.

When Napoleon escaped from Elba, Wellington gave Picton the command of the 5th Infantry Division, and although severely wounded at Quatre Bras he concealed his wound and went to Waterloo. When Napoleon sent in a corps to attack the Anglo-Allied Centre near La Haye Sainte at 13.30, Picton launched a bayonet charge on the advancing French column.

His last words while repulsing the attack with impetuous valour were, 'Charge, charge, Hurrah, Hurrah!' He was shot through the head by a musket ball; he was the highest ranking soldier of Wellington's army to be killed. There were rumours that he was shot by one of his own men and that he had ridden out in his nightshirt and top hat because he had overslept.

He often wore a frock coat into battle. His rather eccentric dress style was one of his eccentricities that made him renowned and the fact that a rumour grew up that he was shot by one of his own men probably meant that his military discipline was rigorous if not brutal.

On June 8th 1859 his body, having been at St George's, Hanover Square was reinterred at St Paul's Cathedral lying closely to the body of Wellington.

After his death at Waterloo, his reputation was high. Colonial frontier towns in Canada, Australia and New Zealand were named in his honour and he remains the only Welshman buried in St Paul's Cathedral. There is an eye catching memorial to him in Carmarthen, it is an imposing stone obelisk and the second on his tomb in the north transept in St Pauls is a bust portraying the Welsh man as a Roman general.

After the end of the war in Spain and he had received his knighthood, he was elected to the House of Commons for one of the Pembroke boroughs and having retired to Wales he was settled as the master of an estate in Carmarthenshire only to be recalled by Wellington and dying a 'glorious' death at Waterloo.

Wellington's Welsh General, the Life of Sir Thomas Picton. Robert Harvard, Aurum Press Ltd, 1996

The Battle of Waterloo Experience. Dan Snow & Peter Snow, Andre Deutsch Ltd, 2015

Lord Raglan

LORD RAGLAN AND CAPTAIN GODFREY MORGAN IN THE CRIMEA

The Raglans, having been descended from the Beauforts, part of the Welsh connection being the birth of Henry Somerset, the 1st Duke of Beaufort were born at Raglan Castle.

The Beauforts had long been associated with Wales, especially in Monmouthshire and on that border. Lord Raglan, later of Crimea fame, was the son of the 5th Duke of Beaufort. He went into the army and served first with the future Duke of Wellington in the peninsula, where he was Wellington's military secretary but his service was not all pen pushing here. He was actively involved in the courageous siege of Badajos. He always had a close relationship with Wellington who admired his politeness, tact and military efficiency.

At Waterloo he acted as the Duke's principal ADC; towards the evening of the third day a musket ball from a sniper on the roof of the farmhouse of La Haye Sainte smashed his right elbow. The surgeon told him to lie down on a table, and then he cut the arm off between the shoulder and the elbow. Lord Raglan did not even murmur. When his arm was tossed away by the surgeon, Raglan called out, *'Hey, bring my arm back! There's a ring my wife gave me on the finger.'*

Although he ran the Board of Ordnance and was considered competent, he had never really commanded troops in battle. The Crimean War was supposed to defend the Turks against the increasing power of the Russians, and especially the Russian ambition to capture Constantinople.

The first blows were struck in the Holy Land where a violent quarrel between the monks of the Roman Catholic Church supported by France and the monks of the Orthodox Church supported by Russia had reached a new bitterness. The Russians it was said at a date a little later had destroyed a Turkish naval flotilla killing 4,000 Turkish sailors, many of them reported to have been shot in the water. France and Britain went to the defence of Turkey.

Lord Raglan had been in the army for nearly half a century, earning respect and affection. He was a trained diplomat and spoke excellent French, and was considered an ideal appointment for the Crimea. His name, mainly as a consequence of a single incident near Balaclava that lasted for twenty minutes has been so well known in the annals of British military history. Because of much of the bungling that went on in the campaign, he has had an extremely bad press; however, his kindness and consideration for others were famous throughout the land. His bravery in battle was never questioned. In the Crimea, like Wellington, he preferred to ride with a single ADC in preference to a cavalcade and chose a frock coat, cravat and cocked hat rather than uniform in the field.

His failure to take Sevastopol, especially when its capture had been announced and celebrated in London during December 1854 lead to further criticisms of the battles of Alma and Inkerman. Historically it is probably Lord Lucan who failed to appreciate the problems of Balaclava and it was he, rather than Raglan, who gave the suicidal order. However, Raglan made an invaluable contribution to the alliance of the armies in the Crimea; his calm personality maintained coherence among the allies and he also insured the independence of the British force despite its numerical inferiority. He was spotless in his private life, honourable and gallant in the field, and was a better general than his critics gave him credit for. As a spotlight on the Battle of Balaclava, we can look at it from the view of a Welshman who was at the front of the charge, Captain Godfrey Morgan.

Captain the Honourable Godfrey Morgan of Lord Tredegar's family set sail for war with the 17th Lancers to the Crimea on 28th March, 1854. The cavalry officer generally cut a great dash; they rode blood horses and were known as 'plungers' or 'tremendous swells' and grew large whiskers and smoked cigars, speaking in a jargon of their own concoction pronouncing 'r' as 'w' and interspersing sentences with a large and meaningless *'Haw haw'*.

The Light Brigade were formed up at the head of the valley before Balaclava, and were ordered by Lord Lucan to advance after a somewhat muddled message from Captain Nolan to Lord Lucan.

There was a mile and a half of ground to cover to the battery of twelve guns to the front which were backed by a mass of Russian cavalry.

Captain Morgan said, *'When we got to about 2 or 300 yards the battery of the Russian Horse artillery opened fire. I do not recollect hearing a word from anybody as we gradually broke from a trot to a canter, although the noise of the striking of men and horses by grape and roundshot was deafening while the dust and gravel struck up by the roundshot that fell short was almost blinding and irritated my horse so that I could scarcely hold him. I appeared to be riding straight onto the muzzle form of the guns and I distinctly saw the gunner apply his fuse. I shut my eyes then for I thought that settled the question as far as I was concerned. But the shot just missed me, and struck the man on my right full in the chest. In another minute I was on the gun and the leading Russian gunhorse, shot I suppose with a pistol by somebody on my right fell across my horse, dragging it over with him and pinning me in between the gun and himself. A Russian gunner on foot had once covered me with his carbine, he was just within reach of my sword and I struck him across the neck. The blow did not do him much harm but it disconcerted his aim. At the same time, a mounted gunner struck my horse on the forehead with his sabre, spurring Sir Briggs, he half jumped, half blundered over the falling horses and then for a short time bolted with me. I only remember finding myself alone amongst the Russians trying to get out as best I could, this by some chance I did in spite of the attempts of the Russians to cut me down. When clear again from the guns, I saw 2 or 3 of my men making their way back and as the fire from both flanks was still heavy, it was a matter of running the gauntlet again. When I was back pretty nearly where we started from, I found that I was the only senior officer of those not wounded and consequently in command'.*

Of the 678 of all ranks that had started, only 195 came back. Sir Briggs is commemorated in the memorial above his grave at Tredegar Park. Godfrey Morgan became ill with fever and was gazetted out of the army, although the fighting had made him a changed man without more stomach for war.

The Destruction of Lord Raglan. Christopher Hibbert, Penguin Books, 1985

Raglan, John Sweetman. Pen & Sword Military, 2010

The Archives of Tredegar House

Private Williams VC

RORKE'S DRIFT AND THE ZULU WARS

Following service in Canada and America, during the campaign for independence, the 24th Regiment was instructed in 1782 to style itself the 24th (2[nd]Warwickshire) Regiment of Foot and it was under this title that the regiment was known for the next 100 years.

In June 1801, the 24th Regiment was sent to Egypt to reinforce the British force fighting the French. They arrived to take part in the capture of Alexandria which ended the campaign and were awarded the Sphinx superscribed Egypt which became the collar badge of the regiment. It took part in Wellington's great victories in Spain where it distinguished itself at Talavera in July 1809. On 22nd January 1879 the 1st and 2nd Battalions were sent out to the Zulu War.

On 12th January 1879, after King Cetshwayo of the Zulus had refused to accept the British ultimatum, British Forces under Command of General Lord Chelmsford invaded Zululand. When the Centre Column advanced across the Myinyathi (Buffalo) River, it left behind on the Natal bank a small garrison, consisting of B Company of the 2nd Battalion 24th Regiment, under the command of Lieutenant Bromhead and a company of the 2nd Battalion 3rd Natal Contingent to secure its depot at Rorke's Drift.

Not anticipating a Zulu attack, the British neglected to fortify the Swedish mission church and house at the place, which had been converted into a commissariat store and a temporary hospital.

The progress of the invading troops was slow owing to the poor weather. On 20th January, Lord Chelmsford, moving with the Centre Column, reached a campsite at the eastern base of Isandhlwana hill.

Meanwhile at Rorke's Drift, some 10 miles away, the men of B Company carried on with their duties of building an enclosure around the post and several Royal Engineers, under the command of Lieutenant Chard, who was now the senior officer at the post, were building a punt across the river.

At first there seemed to be no danger, despite the sound of sporadic gunfire, which the wind carried around the Shiyane (Oskarberg) mountain that lay between Rorke's Drift and Isandhlwana.

Shortly after 3pm on 22nd January, the Hlubi troop of the Natal Native Horse, and other mounted fugitives from Isandhlwana, brought word that over 1,700 soldiers, including native troops, had been annihilated at Isandhlwana by an attacking Zulu force and that a wing of the Zulu army was now on its way towards Rorke's Drift.

Lieutenant Bromhead and Lieutenant Chard immediately set about building a makeshift barricade out of anything that came to hand, wagons, mealie bags and biscuit boxes.

A rough perimeter, incorporating the two buildings was built by the garrison, but the news of the defeat at Isandhlwana was too much for the contingent of native soldiers under the command of Captain George Stephenson. He and the whole contingent fled leaving just 105 soldiers and 36 patients in the hospital to defend themselves against an onslaught of 4,500 Zulus. Chard realised he now was reduced even further.

Within one hour of the news of the disaster at Isandhlwana reaching Chard, the first shot fired out in the defence of Rorke's Drift as the huge Zulu force arrived at the mission station.

For 12 hours the Zulus of King Cetshwayo's Ulundi Corps repeatedly assaulted the post before retreating at about 4am on 23rd January, leaving 450 of their comrades dead.

During the struggle a distant room of the hospital had been held for more than an hour by three privates and, when they finally had no ammunition left, the Zulus burst in, and killed one of the men and two patients.

Meanwhile, Private Williams succeeded in knocking a hole in the partition and taking the last two patients through into the next ward, where he found Private Hook. These two men then worked together – one holding the enemy at bayonet point while the other broke through three more partitions – and they were then able to bring eight patients into the inner line of defence.

The attackers repeatedly attacked the post throughout the night, but the defenders beat off the assaults and only seventeen were dead when relief arrived the following morning.

Lieutenants Chard and Bromhead, Privates John Williams and Henry Hook and seven other defenders of Rorke's Drift were awarded the Victoria Cross.

135

It is significant that despite the mythology created by the film *Zulu*, only about 30% of the defenders of Rorke's Drift were Welsh.

Out of the eleven VCs, only three of the men were Welsh which included Private Williams whose real name was Fielding, although he was born in Wales. Private William Jones and Private Robert Jones had defended the hospital to the last, until six out of the seven patients it contained had been removed.

Private William Jones pawned his VC in later years and was unable to redeem it, and his grave in Park Cemetery in Manchester did not record that he was a VC.

He is known after service to have worked in the theatre, re-enacting the defence of Rorke's Drift; he also toured with Buffalo Bill's Wild West Show in the 1880s and in 1910 he was admitted to the workhouse in Manchester for one night having been found wandering the streets. This was a regular occurrence, as he would awake in the night believing that he was back in South Africa and that the Zulus were about to attack.

He obviously suffered from what we would now call post-traumatic stress. Also Private Robert Jones in 1898 complained of headaches and suffered a form of convulsion.

On 6th September, he borrowed his employer's gun stating that he was going to go and shoot crows and a maid later found his body in the garden of his employer's house at Peterchurch. He had shot himself in the mouth. An inquest held the following day returned a verdict of suicide through unsound mind.

Even up to as recently as 1973 on Rorke's Drift day at the Welsh Brigade Depot at Crickhowell soldiers had to stand and listen to a recording of parts of the film.

In many ways it was the 24th's finest hour, but it was not until 1873 that the Regiment started recruiting mainly from the Welsh Border Counties and a permanent depot was established in Brecon.

It was therefore logical in 1881 when the infantry was given territorial titles that the 24th assumed the title of the South Wales Borderers, a title some of its officers were not terribly happy about as Wales was considered on the periphery of the United Kingdom.

The effect of the film *Zulu* consummately directed by the great Welsh patriot Stanley Baker has probably run its course, but it brought to the world's attention the feats of the Welsh warrior, although a lot of the film was myth. Only 3 of the VCs were Welsh, and only about 30% of the men at the drift were Welsh.

The massacre at Isandhlwana the day before partly caused by the inaccessibility of the ammunition boxes was a profound defeat for the British Army by the brave Zulu warriors armed mainly with spears.

There is an argument that the eleven VCs awarded the following day were some sort of compensation and a smokescreen to hide that ignominious defeat. Nevertheless, it was a glorious defence and the Welsh had a part in it.

It is interesting too that the column of Lord Chelmsford's men who kept out of trouble were commanded by Colonel Glyn related to the Breconshire de

Wintons who later became a major general and colonel of the South Wales Borderers.

The Washing of the Spears. Donald R Morris, Book Club Associates London, 1972

The Rorkes's Drift Men. James W Bancroft, Spellmount, 2010

Zulu. Saul David, Penguin Books, 2005

Thomas Jefferson

THE WELSH IN THE WARS IN AMERICA

The Welsh have always been underplayed in the USA and Canada because they are often like chameleons, blending into their new environment; though numbers were less than the Irish and the Scots, they have made a huge contribution.

The Presidents of Welsh stock were John Adams, James Garfield, William Harrison, James Madison, Thomas Jefferson, Abraham Lincoln, Richard Nixon, Jefferson Davis, President of the Confederate States of America; Martha the wife of President George Washington came from Welsh stock and Hilary Clinton has Welsh on both sides.

A number of the signatories of the Declaration of Independence were Welsh including William Floyd, Stephen Hopkins, Arthur Middleton, Robert Morris, Francis Lewis and Button Gwinnett, revolutionary Governor of Georgia, a general in the Patriot Corps.

The great banker, J P Morgan, was of Welsh stock, as was William Penn, Frank Lloyd Wright and Elihu Yale whose money founded Yale University.

In the military field, a number of Welsh Americans occupied important positions in the War of Independence.

Three grandsons of immigrants, Francis Nash, John Cadwallader and the renowned Daniel Morgan served as generals in the Revolutionary Army.

In 1771, Nash was appointed captain of the militia and in 1775 he became Lt Col and was promoted to general by congress on February 5th, 1777 when he took charge of all the nine regiments of the North Carolina Brigade. His units assisted George Washington to withstand the British after the Battle of Brandywine, Pennsylvania in 1777.

In the Battle of Germantown, Pennsylvania on October 4th the same year he was hit by a cannonball and had to have his leg amputated.

John Cadwallader was born in Philadelphia and was descended from a John Cadwallader from Llanfor, Merionethshire. During the Battle of Lexington 1775 he was in charge of a company of volunteers known as the Silk Stocking Company, and later he was given a commission of Brigadier General under the provincial government, and during the winter campaigns of 1776-7 he was in charge of Pennsylvania's soldiers. Washington described Cadwallader as a man of ability, a good disciplinarian, firm in his principles and of intrepid bravery.

He served at the Battle of Brandywine, Germantown and Monmouth and fought a duel with General Thomas Conway in Philadelphia on July 22nd, 1778. Conway was a troublemaking Irish Frenchman who had been insolent about Washington; Cadwallader's bullet hit Conway in the mouth. Thomas Payne wrote an epitaph to him:

To General John Cadwallader who died February 10th, 1786

At Shrewsbury, his seat in Kent County
In the 44th Year of his age
This amiable, worthy gentleman
Had served his country
With reputation
In the character of a soldier and a statesman
He took an active part and had a principal
Share in the late revolution;
And although he was zealous in the cause
Of American freedom
His conduct was not marked with the
Least degree of malevolence or party spirit
Those who honestly differ from him in opinion
He always treated with singular tenderness.
In sociability and cheerfulness of temper
Honesty and goodness of heart
Independence of spirit and warmth of friendship
He had no superior
And very few equals
Never did any man die more lamented
By his friends and neighbours
To his family and near relations
His death was a stroke still more severe

Daniel Morgan was the victor in the Battle of Cowpens; he again was a ferocious fighter. At the time of the Civil War, there were up to 200,000 Welsh speaking people in Pennsylvania, Central New York, Sothern Wisconsin, Central Ohio and Iowa.

There was also a sizeable settlement in South Carolina, and there was a Welsh tract along the Cape Fear River in North Carolina.

Although the Welsh were concentrated in certain places, there were not enough in any one area to raise a regiment to fight under the red dragon banner. But there were small company sized units of 100 men like the COG 77th Pennsylvania and COE 97th New York, which were mostly Welsh.

Other regiments such as the 117th and 146th New York, 23rd Wisconsin, 9th Minnesota, 50th, 76th, 115th, 117th and 118th Ohio had large numbers of Welshmen.

The famous Pennsylvania's 48th regiment had many Welsh coal miners who were responsible for mining under rebel trenches. There were few native Welshmen in Confederate service, but there were many Southern soldiers who had Welsh names.

There were only two Welsh born generals, and they both served the North. Brigadier William Powell came from Pontypool in Gwent; he served in the Union cavalry in West Virginia and won the Congressional Medal of Honour at Sinking Creek. He was active against the famous 'Grey Ghost', John S Moseby, and hanged a number of Moseby's rangers.

Brigadier General Joshua Owen was born in Carmarthen and despite his Welsh origins, his nickname was 'Paddy' as he commanded an Irish regiment at the beginning of the war. He was promoted to general for gallantry at the Battle of Glendale but his failure to support other troops at Coldharbour led to his being disciplined for disobedience. Many distinguished generals of both sides were of Welsh blood; Confederate General 'Grumble' Jones proudly claimed descent from Welsh princes. General James Rice's Brigade fought hand to hand with those of Junius Daniel.

Other Welsh American generals on the field included Union chief of staff Andrew Humphreys, Simon Griffin and Henry Thomas. Facing them were Benjamin Humphreys, Edward Thomas, Thomas Rosser, Micah Jenkins and Robert Rhodes.

The true heroes of any war are obviously the common soldiers and worthy officers.

At least eight Welshmen won the Congressional Medal of Honour, while on the other side of the ledger only one was executed by a military court. As befitting a nation whose elegies were often directed to the spiritual, a chaplain of Welsh descent, Captain Horatio Howell of the 90th Pennsylvania was immortalised at Gettysberg as the only chaplain to be killed by hostile fire.

The Welsh were hardly wilting lilies or wallflowers in either the Civil War or the War of Independence. The last part of this essay is a discussion of the Welsh Regiment's part in the Anglo American War of 1812.

The honour on the colour of the 41st Welsh Regiment was called Miami for the actions fought along the banks of the Miami River in the area of Fort Maigs, an American stronghold in Ohio State, North America.

A force under the command of General Proctor including 500 men of the 41st Regiment, a combined British and Canadian force sailed down the Detroit River and across Lake Erie, arriving at the mouth of the Miami River in late April, 1813.

The American batteries were eventually stormed and 450 prisoners were captured. The 41st lost eleven rank and file killed, and one officer and three sergeants wounded. With great help from the natives, the Americans were defeated at the Battle of Warbash; the war was to rage both on land and the great lakes for another year in which men of both the 1st and the 2nd battalions of the 41st played a major part.

Other battle honours were awarded for Detroit, Queenstown Heights and Niagra. It could be said that the 41st or Welsh regiment were particularly instrumental in keeping the Americans out of Canada; thus on the north American continent the Welsh were involved in three wars, The American war of Independence, the American Civil War and the American Canadian War.

As well as the Welsh Regiment, serving from Lexington Green in 1775 to York Town in 1781, one regiment marched thousands of miles and fought a dozen battles to uphold British rule in America, the Royal Welsh Fusiliers. Along the way they promoted new tactics and appointed new leaders which together laid the foundations for the subsequent victory over Napoleon.

The Welsh, as well as being rebels, could be the most loyal of troops and the RWF are known for their loyalty so deeply that the monarch has given them permission not to stand for the Loyal Toast.

Americans from Wales. Edward G Hartmann, Ph.D, Octagon Books, New York, 1983

150 Famous Welsh Americans. W Arvon Roberts, Gwasg Carreg Gwalch, 2000

Sir Hugh Rowlands VC

GENERAL SIR HUGH ROWLANDS VC IN THE TRANSVAAL

Sir Hugh Rowlands VC was born in 1828 into a secure middle class and strongly Welsh environment in the village of Llanrug. His father was a member of a minor country gentry family and was the heir of Hugh Rowlands of Ty Mawr, Llanddurog, steward to the estate of the local magnate Lord Newborough.

The Rowlands family claimed descent from Blethyn ap Cynfyn the 11th century prince of Powys. Hugh, the future general, loved his country, was proud of being a Welshman and spoke the language throughout his life. By 1846, he had reached a decision about his future career and applied for a position in the army.

Through some patronage, hard earned, he was offered the rank of ensign in the 41st Regiment of Foot which became the Welch Regiment. He was known to be passionately fond of horses throughout his life and a very proficient horseman. He did not attempt to enter the cavalry and, although the 41st was designated the Welch Regiment, it was composed mainly of Irishmen.

For him the army was not to be a temporary means of passing a few years until he came into his inheritance for it was unlikely that he would inherit the Plastirion Estate; it was to be a full time career.

151

With the advent of the Crimean War, the 41st Regiment of Foot had received their orders to stand by for active service in March, 1854. The 41st disembarked from the 'City of London' ship on 14th September; the regiment had a strength of 25 officers and about 930 men.

At the Battle of Alma on 20th September the 41st were ordered to advance and, in later years, Rowlands recalled his feelings as he waited to go into action for the first time. His nerves began to affect him and he felt butterflies in his stomach. Suddenly he heard a voice call out in Welsh from somewhere in the rear. 'Rwan yr Hen Blastirion! Rwan ambiff' ('Now old Plastirion! Now for a fight').

It was a man named Lovell who came from Tan Yr Allt, Llanrhug and who was also serving in the regiment. The realisation that he was being watched and that the honour of his family was at stake caused him to calm himself for his first taste of the realities of war.

Rowlands described the advance of his men up the slope,' *We advanced in double columns of companies from the centres of divisions with artillery on our flanks and a strong line of skirmishers in front of all. On nearing them we deployed into line, the men remarkably steady under fire of shot and shell from a battery on a high hill. The 41st right wing joined with the French left and all did their job admirably driving them from their position in 4 hours and a half*.

Rowlands went on to fight at the Battle of Inkerman where on 24th February, 1857 he was cited for a Victoria Cross for having rescued Colonel Haly of the 47th regiment from Russian soldiers who had wounded and surrounded him and for gallant exertions in holding the ground occupied by his advance picket against the enemy at the commencement of the Battle of Inkerman. He was nominated for a second VC for his action during the abortive attack on Redan on 18th June 1855.

Life in the Crimean winter of 1855-6 was far more comfortable than that of the previous year. A peace treaty was signed in Paris on 17th June. The 41st regiment marched from its camp to the port of Kameish where it boarded the transport ship 'Transit' for the passage home to Britain. Rowlands returned home to a tumultuous welcome.

Not since the return of the 1st Marquis of Anglesey from Waterloo had northwest Wales had a local military hero. On 23rd March, 1866 at the age of 38, Hugh Rowlands was promoted to Lt Colonel and became commanding officer of the 41st of Foot.

He was stationed in India and had a bride to be who was 21 years his junior. Both families were gentry in Caernarvonshire.

The average age for promotion to the rank of Lt Colonel during the mid 19th century was 49, he reached the rank at 38.

On its return to Britain, the Welch Regiment as it was being called by the 1870s was stationed in Shorncliffe and after 26 years' service with the Welch Regiment he left to command the 1st Battalion the Border Regiment which was about to go to India. He had got to the end of his command of the 34th regiment which he felt was a disappointment as they had seen little active service.

As he did not speak any of the native languages of India he was unable to be appointed to the staff. It was at this stage that Lt General Thesiger requested that he be transferred to South Africa. He was appointed Inspector of Colonial Forces. There were various upsets with his superiors which showed that he would rock the boat because of his concern for the men under his command and he would do this despite consequences to himself.

In spite of this, Thesiger had appointed Rowlands to the position of Commandant of the Transvaal. There was plenty of active service at the time, both against the natives and trying to prevent a Boer uprising but despite the author's previous conviction, Rowlands was not one of the instigators of concentration camps.

It is interesting that in a letter that Thesiger wrote to another officer, Sir Theophilus Shepstone, saying *'Rowlands as an independent field commander is a failure. I will not put him in such a position again. I hear that he sits in his tent and writes all day. This will not do in South African warfare. A commander must ride about and see the country himself or he will never be able to handle his troops properly.'*

Rowlands had a few enemies who had worked on the general to suggest the former had lost the confidence of the men under his command but there is little evidence to suggest this was true.

Then came the invasion of Zululand; Thesiger's career as Lord Chelmsford came an awful cropper with the defeat at Isandlwana. Rowlands was appointed on 26th May 1878; he was given a brigade of his own. On 11th July, Rowlands left the coast of the colony where he took command of Fort Chelmsford where he remained until late August, returning to Caernarvon where preparations were in full swing for the National Eisteddfod of Wales.

He attended the Proclamation Ceremony and when he came on to the platform the crowd rose and cheered loudly, waving their hats and the band struck up, *'Hail, the conquering hero comes.'*

He had reverted to the role of colonel on leaving the Cape, but was then appointed Brigadier General to command the Peshawar in the Punjab; however, he was promoted Major General in July 1881 but he returned to Britain in August 1882.

On 21st April 1824, Rowlands was appointed to command the Bangladore Division of the Madras Army, quickly implementing new training programmes for the division and his commander General Roberts was impressed by Rowlands as a man and as a leader.

On 22nd April 1888, he sailed from India for the last time and on New Year's Day 1890 he was promoted to Lt General and became Lieutenant of the Tower of London. At the time of his retirement he was three years short of completing 47 years service.

He returned to the family home Plastirion and immediately set out to make it a successful commercial enterprise. Much of this time was spent devoted to his duties as Justice of the Peace, serving as the chairman of the Caernarvon bench. He served many years as churchwarden of St Michael's Llanrug.

His only son unfortunately died while serving as a major in the Kings African Rifles which almost broke the General's heart.

Here was a great Welshman who had distinguished himself as a great fighting man who had never lost his love for his roots and still retained the ability to speak the language, and is a role model for all us former Welsh soldiers and a great representative of the Welch Regiment.

Commandant of the Transvaal. W Alister Williams, Bridge Books, Wrexham, 2001

VCs of Wales and the Welsh Regiments. Alister Williams, Bridge Books. 1984

Heart of a Dragon. The VCs of Wales and the Welsh Regiments. Bridge Books, 2006

Brigadier Llewellyn Price-Davies VC

THE WELSH VCs IN THE FIRST WORLD WAR

The first personality we deal with is Brigadier General Lewis Pugh Evans VC. He was born at the old Abermard house near Llanilar. He came from an old Welsh family that could trace its roots back to the second Royal tribe of Wales. His father was knighted for his work as a member of the Legislative Council on the governing body of British India. He was one of seven children and part of a very large family. He was educated at Eton where he proved a hard worker and was top of his form. He went to the Royal Military Academy at Sandhurst, preparing to join the Royal Welsh Fusiliers but he was offered a commission in the Black Watch which he took because he could go straight out to the African War and active service. There, he took part in numerous operations and was captured for a short time by the Boers.

He came back to England in 1908, and there he learned to fly one of the early aeroplanes. He started off in World War 1 with the newly formed Royal Flying Corps, but later returned to the Black Watch as a company commander where he earned his first DSO.

In 1917 he became commanding officer of the 1st Lincolnshire Regiment and it was at this time that he was awarded the Victoria Cross when he personally led his men on a vital mission that was accomplished, but at great cost.

Of the 22 officers and 570 men who set out, only four officers including him and 160 men made it to the final objective. The official citation for the Victoria Cross read as follows:

'For most conspicuous bravery and leadership, Lt Col Evans took his battalion in perfect order through terrific enemy barrage, personally formed up all units and led them to the assault while a strong machine gun placement was causing casualties and the troops were working around the flank, Lt Col Evans rushed at it himself and by firing his revolver through the loophole, forced the emplacement to capitulate.

After capturing the first objective he was severely wounded in the shoulder but refused to be bandaged and reformed the troops, pointed out all future objectives and again led his battalion forward.

Again badly wounded, he nevertheless continued to command until the second objective was won and after consolidation collapsed from loss of blood. As there were numerous casualties, he refused assistance and by his own efforts ultimately reached the dressing station.

His example of cool bravery stimulated in all ranks the highest valour and determination to win'.

After a spell in hospital he was back in action, in command of the 1st Battalion of the Black Watch. During this period, he was awarded his second DSO and once again he was in the thick of battle, leading from the front. In September 1926 he returned to command the 2nd Battalion of the Black Watch.

One of his contemporaries said, 'We knew him as an extremely quiet, polite and modest senior officer. Many of us were apprehensive that he would be too reserved for the job, but within days of his assumption of the command he started to take charge and shake everything into proper shape.'

He lost his wife in a railway accident in 1921 but returned to his beloved 'Loves Grove', an estate which he inherited in 1945. He declined the exacting post of Lord Lieutenant for Carmarthenshire, and his Jersey cattle were his abiding farming interest; he kept many mountain sheep on the slopes of Plynlimon.

During these years he was assisted by two sisters, and, latterly, two nieces as well as an excellent estate staff, many of whom had spent their entire working life with the family. Death came suddenly while travelling by train to London in 1962. He was 81.

There was another Major General Lewis Pugh whom R S Thomas, the great poet, first encountered in his parish in Machynlleth. He was a war hero, awarded the DSO three times, a man who could speak German, Urdu and Ghurkale and had crossed the northwest frontier in disguise.

Of all the potential enemies he could have chosen in the world, Thomas had to pick on him. He was played by Gregory Peck in the film 'The Sea Wolves' and was not the usual caricature of a general. Physically, he and Thomas were not dissimilar. They were of an age, both very tall, austere men though Pugh had a monocle. Both he and Thomas were intelligent, complex men, both spoke English with cut glass accents, but both took being Welsh very seriously. Pugh who had spoken Welsh as a child, enrolled in his retirement at a further education class in Aberystwyth, sitting among youngsters so he could take a GCE in it.

Vicar and General would have had a lot in common. However, one was a pacifist given to agonising in print over his possible cowardice. The other was a courageous war hero. Lewis, a Welshman who had become English and a general, and R S Thomas, an Englishman who had become Welsh. Thomas's sermons in particular did not suit Lewis because he felt they were all doom and gloom. Lewis would often talk about Thomas and usually say something like, 'That nutter'.

Brigadier Llewellyn Price-Davies was commissioned into the King's Royal Rifle Corps. His place of birth was Marrington Hall, Chirbury, Shropshire. He was educated at Marlborough school and served in the Boer War. He was GOC of the 38th Welsh Division December 1915 – Dec 1917.

He won his VC at Blood River Port, S Africa on 17th September 1901 when the Boers had overwhelmed the right of the British column and some 400 of them were galloping round the flank and rear of the guns, riding up to the drivers (who were trying to get the guns away) and calling upon them to surrender.

Lt Price-Davies, hearing an order to fire upon the charging Boers, immediately drew his revolver and dashed upon them in a gallant and most desperate attempt to rescue the guns. He was at once shot and knocked off his horse but was not mortally wounded, although he had ridden to what seemed to be almost certain death without a moment's hesitation.

162

It is very interesting that the poet David Jones bumped into Price-Davies in the trenches. Price-Davies was slim, handsome, obstinately fastidious and spoke slowly and primly. Behind his back his fellow officers called him 'Jane'. He wore a unique, completely waterproof outfit resembling a pair of overalls, which Jones thought very nice and eminently practical for endlessly wet trench life.

Once, when Jones was on sentry duty, Price-Davies appeared around the travis of a fire bay; he was carrying his wooden staff 4 feet 6 inches long which was the regulation height of the fire step of the parapet above the fire step. He determined that this was an inch of so over the regulation height and ordered Jones and those present to make the adjustment.

Price-Davies was imperturbable, ignoring rifle fire, machine gun fire, shrapnel and even heavy bombardment. Jones saw him several times, fully exposing himself to fire in the daylight in order to measure the level of sandbags.

The men thought him stupid. During a heavy barrage with his subordinate officers, they were unable to run for cover without him; he was seen to be carefully undoing a package and saying, *'I so hate to waste string, especially in wartime.'* When he got it open he complained, *'When will my aunt learn that what I like is chocolate, not chocolates?'*

The burial of tins was a special concern of his. He ordered Jones' battalion once to collect so many tins that they filled 600 sandbags, taking the battalion a week to do this.

Once, when a Welsh battalion passed through a communication trench towards the front singing the brooding, melancholy hymns they generally sang, Jones heard Price-Davies ask one of his officers, *'Why do they sing such sad songs that sound like hymns? It's bad for morale, very bad'*. David Jones was dismayed by his insensitivity.

John Collins VC

John Collins was born in Somerset in 1877. By 1890 he was living in Penydaren, working as a collier in the Bedlinog Colliery until the war began. Collins had fought for the army in South Africa; as soon as the call for soldiers went out, Collins re-enlisted and became a corporal in the Welsh Horse 25th Battalion Royal Welsh Fusiliers.

He was awarded the Victoria Cross for his actions at Beershegba in Palestine on October 31st 1917. Prior to an attack, his battalion was forced to lie out in the open under heavy shell and machine gun fire which caused many casualties. Collins repeatedly went out under heavy fire and brought wounded back to cover, thus saving many lives.

In subsequent operations throughout the day Corporal Collins was conspicuous in rallying and leading his command. He led the final assault with the utmost skill in spite of heavy fire at close range and uncut wire.

He bayoneted 15 of the enemy and with the Lewis Gun section pressed on with the objective.

Isolated and under fire from snipers and guns, he showed throughout a magnificent example of initiative and fearlessness. A few months later, he was awarded the Distinguished Conduct Medal, when through his gallantry he helped 80 of the Welsh Horse take 300 Turkish prisoners with their machine guns destroyed. After this action he was promoted to sergeant.

After all this courage shown by these men, it is interesting to remember the life of Sir Owen Thomas M P. His military service commenced with service with the 2nd Volunteer Battalion the Royal Welsh Fusiliers in the late 1880s. Service in the Boer War saw Thomas raise his own mounted infantry regiment, The Prince of Wales Light Horse, complete with his own twelve year old son enrolled as a bugler.

The call to arms by Lord Kitchener and David Lloyd George's desire to raise a Welsh army corps led to Thomas being appointed the Commander for the North Wales Pals Brigade, later 113th Brigade, 38th Welsh Division.

Whilst his training methods can be seen as outdated, his greatest contribution was to persuade significant numbers of men from North Wales to enlist despite the tradition of Nonconformism. Sadly, this included all three of his own sons, all of whom were to be killed serving with the RWF and the RFC. Bitter disappointment was to follow his efforts to raise and train the N Wales Brigade when he was denied command on active service due to his age.

This group of men were all an exemplary collection of Welshmen who served their country with huge courage and fortitude.

There is a partial theme on the Merthyr contribution running through the book, but to add to this, as the author is having a book launch in Merthyr, he shows two memorials at Cyfarthfa Grammar School for the First and Second World War. There is a further memorial there to Squadron Leader Ecclestone who won an AFC and a DFC.

CYFARTHFA CASTLE SCHOOL

ERECTED BY THE OLD STUDENTS ASSOCIATION
IN PROUD MEMORY OF THOSE WHO FELL SERVING WITH
HIS MAJESTY'S FORCES AND AUXILIARY UNITS IN THE
SECOND WORLD WAR. 1939-1945

VALMAI ALDERSON	B. HENNESSEY	W. T. JONES	T. J. O'SULLIVAN	F. STEVENS
W. F. AMOS	T. W. HILL	G. J. A. KENVIN	R. D. OWEN (STAFF)	A. THOMAS
D. T. ANTHONY	E. HITCHINS	A. I. MACNAUGHT	G. PEARSON	J. E. THOMAS
R. BEYNON	I. J. HUGHES	W. MAYO	W. T. PHILLIPS	R. THOMAS
F. V. BORD	C. JAMES	E. McCARTHY	D. PRICE	W. J. WALSH
W. L. CLEARY	T. S. JAMES	C. I. MEREDITH	T. PULLIN	N. WEGENER
T. A. DAVIES	T. W. JAMES	D. G. MORGAN	E. D. REES	K. WILLIAMS
W. R. S. DAVIES	C. JONES	E. D. MORGANS	G. REYNOLDS	N. D. WILLIAMS
E. J. EVANS	M. L. JONES	J. H. MORGAN	P. ROTHWELL	W. P. WILLIAMS
I. GRIFFITHS	R. JONES	A. MORRIS	A. B. SOLARI	R. WOODHOUSE
R. OLIVER		D. G. O'SULLIVAN		H. THOMAS

See previous chapter for Bibliography, also

The Letters of Major General Price Davies VC. Peter Robinson, The History Press, 2013

The Archives of Aberystwyth University for Brigadier General Lewis Pugh Evans

The Long Conversation, a Memoir of David Jones. William Blissett. Western Printing Services, 1981

David Jones in the Great War. Thomas Dilworth, Enitharmon, 2012

168

T.E.Lawrence

LAWRENCE OF ARABIA

He was born in 1888 in Tremadog, North Wales. His father was Anglo-Irish. Ivor Wynne Jones, author and journalist, has done some research on his mother. Ivor said, when he was chatting in a mixture of Irish and Arabic to an Howeitat chieftain in the Negev somewhere North of Aqaba, 'I told him I was not 'chaskari Ingilizi' but came from Wales', not expecting much response from a desert Bedouin. To my surprise, he said, 'Ah, the same country as Major Lawrence'. More surprising than the Arab's response was the fact that T. E. L. had ever bothered to make the point after leading the poor Hashemites out of the Hejaz into a stateless wilderness.

In his research Ivor Wynne Jones says that he came to disregard the information on T. E. L.'s mother's birth certificate and found that his grandfather on his mother's side was John Lawrence born in Monmouth, the son of a Swansea-born mother and a Monmouth-born father. That also gives the origin of the surname 'Lawrence' which, otherwise, would appear to have been plucked out of the air by a father called 'Chapman' and a mother named 'Junar'. You also get the origin of Sarah Junar's Christian name, Sarah Lawrence, who was the mother of Sarah Junar's young father.

In his early boyhood at about the age of five, the family moved from Trebanog to Oxford where he attended

Oxford High School. He chose Jesus College as his second choice when trying for Oxford, mainly because he was awarded a Meyricke exhibition to this Welsh College which was a Welsh exhibition which he qualified for by his Welsh birthplace.

From early childhood Lawrence was devoted to books and the subject matter was often castles, especially the medieval history surrounding them and their architecture. He also soon began to take a considerable interest in warfare, both ancient and modern. He was gifted with a terrific memory for detail, especially for countries and their people. Behind all this interest there was a deep introspection and self-consciousness according to his friend Vyvyan Richards.

One of his great qualities was a tremendous attachment to personal freedom and the equality of the individual. He was never at college or at school a team man but he certainly wasn't a bookworm. He was an adventurer and, even at Oxford, explored parts other people did not know existed. Even at this stage in his career he also slept and ate less than most other people. Not only was he a man of learning but he had remarkable skill with his hands. He always mended things and fine printing was one of the activities that most appealed to him.

His attachment to the Ashmolean Museum inspired him to explore the Middle East. Regarding his attachment to Wales and his Welshness, I note that he was said once to have claimed that he came from one of the few countries that had beaten England.

Lawrence, having had much experience in the Middle East, was commissioned near the outbreak of war on

172

October 23, 1914. He was a temporary 2nd Lt interpreter and became involved in intelligence.

We now come to his relationship with the Arabs.

The state of oppression they had suffered under the Turks made a deep impression on him. He wanted to become their champion and rescue a whole people from slavery. In all his affairs, personal affection was one of his highest attributes. He had a number of close and young Arab friends but there was never any evidence that relationships were permeated by physical homosexuality.

He soon realised the economic life of the desert was based on the supply of camels which were best nurtured in the hill pastures. This moulded the life of the Bedouin who travelled between the Spring, Summer and Winter pasturages. He realised the Bedouin were a people of black and white whose thoughts tended to dwell on extremes. The sense of freedom that the roaming Bedouin gave to Lawrence and the harshness of their existence which appealed to his aesthetic side made him their great companion. He saw them as unstable as water but, like water, they would eventually take over.

For a whole year and more from the capture of Aqaba in July 1917 to the capture of Damascus in October 1918 Lawrence had the huge and exacting job of knitting together the wild Bedouin and the trained forces of the British. Lawrence learned very quickly how to accommodate the Arabs. He described their gatherings of chieftains as something between wolves and wayward children and he subtly directed their ideas and learnt their individual foibles.

For Lawrence the training and movement across the desert were the most thrilling part of the campaign. The gore and nastiness of the slaughter the Arabs imposed on the Turks he was not keen on. There was an incident with a Turkish official which could have been described as homosexual rape after he was captured but to this day we do not know the truth of the details. As for the inspiration which drove him to write 'The Seven Pillars of Wisdom' there was certainly not much Christian spirituality behind it as he had always certainly dismissed conventional Christianity, having had it forced down his throat by his mother. There is no doubt that he was a man of deep spiritual feeling. Much of it came from nature especially the desert. I have seen nowhere reports that he embraced Islam.

He left Arabia, initially dejected at what he saw was the betrayal of the Arabs by the great powers but, when eventually a separate Arab kingdom was created, he felt he had been justified and a lot of the struggle had been worth it. He did not want to be lauded in his native kingdom of Britain but preferred instead to become a lowly aircraftman in the RAF. He was delighted and excited by new technologies and machines and this position allowed him access to them. Having been a war hero, a distinguished soldier and in rank a full colonel, he was an embarrassment to the authorities but he believed in personal choice and pursuing his own destiny. This he was allowed to do up to a point.

He wrote his great tome 'Seven Pillars of Wisdom' which made a huge contribution to the history of the campaign. But he was its greatest critic, feeling that it had never achieved greatness as a work of art. He once said a man never amounts to anything unless he be an artist.

No great captain had really portrayed the inner workings of his spirit in the way Lawrence depicted them in this book. From the spiritual point of view, he once said according to his brother the words, 'I hate Christianity' but that never stopped him growing into a great spirit, a great leader of men and a huge inspiration to the Arab people whom he loved and whose freedom he pursued relentlessly.

'Hero, the Life and Legend of Lawrence of Arabia'. Michael Korda

'The Seven Pillars of Wisdom'. T E Lawrence

'Lawrence of Arabia, the Selected Letters'. Edited by Malcolm Brown

David Jones

GHELUVELT AND MAMETZ WOOD

When plans were implemented to augment the strength of the British regular and territorial army, the idea was introduced to raise battalions from within existing communities. As examples, the 16th RWF were originally recruited from employees at the City Hall in Cardiff and the first 1,000 recruits wore the badge of the Cardiff City Coat of Arms.

The 10th and 13th Welsh were recruited from the mining area and became known as the 1st and 2nd Rhondda. The 14th Welsh owe their existence to the Swansea Football and Cricket Club.

Lloyd George proposed to recruit and form a Welsh army of two divisions. Recruitment was slow because so many Welshmen had joined other regiments, but 50,000 were recruited for one division, the 38th. There was a general shortage of officers in all of Kitchener's new armies and many officers were brought out of retirement and some of these had only limited experience.

Lloyd George also involved himself in the personal recruitment of a number of senior officers, which did not go down very well with Kitchener. The 29th October 1914 was the first of the five days when the Kaiser was present in person with his troops opposite Ypres, hoping his presence would stimulate an irresistible breakthrough.

The Germans had brought in a new army group full of well trained and experienced troops. Their arrival meant that the allies 11 and a half divisions now faced 23 and a half German divisions. The Germans also had 260 heavy Howitzers and mortars in addition to 184 smaller calibre guns.

Meanwhile some smaller British artillery units had been removed from the front owing to a shortage of shells. Lieutenant Colonel Henry Cadogan commanded 1 RWF who were so depleted that six officers had to be sent up on attachment to him.

Cadogan's men had taken up positions in trenches in full view of the enemy. They could only retire over an exposed slope. His men were in a death trap. The Royal Welsh's position was further weakened in the middle by a big gap where the road from Zandvoorde to Becelaere passed through.

British intelligence did not really realise what was about to happen to them. It was a misty morning in the autumn on 30th. At 6am a tremendous battle took place on the crossroads south of Gheluvelt. Trenches were taken and retaken. A huge bombardment opened up on Hal or Henry's battalion and then the massed infantry attacked. The battalion had been under heavy artillery fire for 3 hours. Henry issued the order to stay in their trenches; a retreat would have spelled disaster.

The Germans brought forward a battery onto the high ground on the edge of the village. This opened up with shrapnel raking the battalion's trenches from end to end. Our men began to run out of ammunition and their rifles began to jam.

The enemy had reached a position on the flank of the Welsh Fusiliers. The regiment's position was hopeless; its right flank and its own trenches were completely unprotected. The regiment fought until every officer had been killed or wounded. Only 90 men re-joined the brigade. The adjutant Lt Dooner was killed in a very gallant attempt to cross the interval which divided the trenches and investigate the state of affairs on the right.

The colonel fell in an equally gallant attempt to rescue his subordinate after he had fallen. Ten officers and 320 NCOs and men had disappeared after the battle. Only 86 men answered the roll call that evening. Of the missing, only four officers and 50 men were found to be prisoners, every one of whom had been wounded by a splinter or bullet. The balance, 275 of them were dead.

This was a terrible battle and another one was Mametz Wood, when the 38th Welsh division commanded by General Lloyd and particularly 115 Brigade commanded by Brigadier General H J Evans saw action.

Soon after, the British artillery began their bombardment at 8am on 7th July 1816; as soon as the leading waves of the 16th Welsh came over the crest of the slope they were hit by heavy machine gun fire; the casualties were enormous. On the left, the 11th S W Borderers pushed forwards through the valley but were also pushed back by intense machine frontal machine gun fire. Soon afterwards, the 10th S W Borderers were also thrown into the attack.

Brigadier General Evans went forward and found the attacking battalion no closer to the wood than 250 yards, partially dug in and somewhat disorganised. Captain Griffith who was with him observed that men were burrowing into the ground with their entrenching tools, seeking whatever cover they might take. Wounded men were crawling back from the ridge and men were crawling forward with ammunition. No attack could succeed over such ground, as this was swept by short range weapons from the front and the side.

Brigadier General Evans was subject to much criticism for delaying attacks which headquarters wanted to go in because he feared more devastating casualties. Much more devastating fighting went on around Mametz Wood, and further attacks did proceed.

The wood was eventually taken and the total number of casualties sustained by the 38th Welsh Division were 46 officers and 556 other ranks killed, six officers and 579 other ranks missing, and 138 officers and 2,668 other ranks wounded.

Captain Llewelyn Wyn Griffith talked about how before the division had attempted to capture Mametz Wood, it was known that, 'the undergrowth in it was so dense that it was all but impossible to move through it. Years of neglect had turned the wood into a formidable barrier; heavy shelling of the southern end had beaten down some of the young growth but it had also thrown the largest trees and branches into a barricade.

There were more corpses than men, but there were worse sights than corpses limbs and mutilated trunks, here and there, a detached head forming splashes of red among the green leaves.

An advertisement of the horror of our way of life and death and of our crucifixion of youth one tree held in its branches a leg with its torn flesh hanging down over a spray of leaf. Even now, after all these years, this round ring of manmade hell bursts into my vision', says Wyn Griffith, 'Elbowing into an infinity of distance the wall of my room dwarfing into nothingness objects we call real. Blue sky above a band of green trees and a ploughed graveyard in which living men moved wormlike in and out of sight.'

These two terrible battles exemplified the courage and stubbornness of the Welsh.

It was from some of these actions that came the great fount of Welsh poetry by Hedd Wyn, David Jones and two Englishmen in the Royal Welch Fusiliers, Robert Graves and Siegfreid Sassoon. This has immortalised the bravery of the Welsh soldier.

The Road to Armageddon. Edited by Colonel Henry Cadogan RWF, HMEC, Wales, 2014

The Welsh at Mametz Wood. The Somme 1916. Jonathan Hicks, Y Lolfa Cyf, Wales, 2016

Up to Mametz. Wyn Griffith, Gliddon Books, 1988

The Welsh in the Spanish civil war

THE WELSH IN THE SPANISH CIVIL WAR

Spain was a cauldron in the 1930's. The Republicans on the left had been radical in their approach to land reform and had undermined the privileges of the entrenched class system. Their reforms were too much for the old establishment.

The landed aristocracy, the army and the higher clergy rose in defence of their positions of special privileges and political preferment. They managed to regain control through the ballot box in 1933. They immediately set about driving the peasants off the land and burning their crops. They restored to the clergy political power and control of the schools and they re-established the old privileges of the officer's caste, overturning much of the reforms.

There was an uprising by the miners of Northern Asturis in northern Spain which was ruthlessly repressed. However, in February 1936 the parties of the Popular Front won power back.

On 17th July 1936 a coup led by General Franco was staged and the Civil War began. There were 5 principal areas of conflict – the distribution and ownership of the land; authoritarianism v libertarianism; the power of the church and its relationship with the state; traditional gender roles v the new woman and national government v regional independence.

The Nazis in Germany and Fascists in Italy came to help Franco, although Britain which had signed the non-intervention agreement of February 1937 failed to aid the Republicans. In Wales, both those in the Communist party of Great Britain and the S W Miners Federation supported the Republican government. Collections were made throughout Wales for the Republicans.

Captain David John (*Potato*) Jones became a Civil War legend for his services to supply the Republican governments needs for food, fuel and medical supplies. His Welsh craft ferried as many as 25,000 refugees from Franco's bombing of Basque and other towns.

The Basques in particular were against Franco and the almost total destruction by Nazi war planes of Guernica on market day on 26th April 1937 is the first ever mass bombing of civilians and was thus a hugely symbolic act, a conscious attack on the very heart of Basque regionalism and all it stood for.

Many from the free world flocked to join the International Brigade to fight for the Republicans, the exact number of people who went from Wales is unknown. Hywel Francis claims the number to be 174, others suggest 200. William Rust in his 1939 book, 'Britons in Spain' lists just 21 Welsh dead, others believe it was 34.

Volunteering was illegal, so many men had to leave for Spain secretly without telling their families. It was reported that the Welsh volunteers raised the morale of the Spanish civilians and the other Republican troops by their unity, their tenacity and in particular their singing.

The miners tunnelling skills were also useful.

There was huge support in the Valleys for the Republican cause; large sums of money were raised and it was the people from these mining communities that made up the majority of those that went to fight. 118 of them came from the S W coalfield and had received their education in miners' institute libraries.

An estimated 35,000 men and women came from some 50 nations from all corners of the globe to fight for the Republicans. Conditions were far from ideal for the International Brigades. Will Paynter, one of the Welsh volunteers, talked about desperate lack of working weapons and ammunition, little or no training, poor leadership, mental and physical exhaustion, inadequate food rations and clothing, low morale and high mortality.

Edwin Greening from Aberamman said about the International Brigades, 'You are a true worker intellectual combining thought and action for the benefit of your community and the whole of humanity. You strove all your life to achieve what Paul Robeson called, "Dignity and abundance for all"'.

Alan Menai Williams served as a paramedic on the battleground at every major battle, giving emergency first aid to the wounded and arranging their transport to the field hospital. He was himself wounded at Brunete, but was at the front again within three weeks. To escape the advancing Nationalist Army, Alan with six of his comrades swam the Ebro River under machine gun fire. Only four, including Williams, made it to the other side.

Of the 331 volunteers in the ranks of the British Battalion at the start of the Battle of Brunete, only 24 remained alive or uninjured after a week's fierce fighting.

Harry Dobson from Blaenclydach served with distinction at the Battles of Brunete, Quinto, Belchite, Mediana, Huesca, Teruel, Caspe and Gandesa. He reached the rank of captain and was wounded by machine gun fire on Hill 481.

The only Welshman to fight on Franco's side was Frank Thomas, a 22 year old commercial traveller who hated Communism. After eight months of fighting, Frank was shot through the jaw, the cheek and the leg. In contrast to the disorganisation of the Republican side, Frank recalls that discipline was very, very strong. On the training ground, Corporals used whips. 'I've seen an officer kick a man because his rifle was dirty'.

At least five Welshmen were killed at the Battle of Jarama in February 1937. According to Bob Cooney, a battalion commissar, it was a baptism of such a fierce and sudden character which was fought under the worst possible conditions.

Early on the morning of 25th July 1938, the 15th International Brigade crossed the Ebro River and launched an attack to try to halt the Nationalist forces who were advancing across Valencia.

It was a bloody battle, fought in temperatures of about 30 degrees Centigrade and involving savage trench warfare in rough and hilly terrain. The brigade were driven back again and again from Hill4 81.

The Republican forces who had little defence against superior enemy artillery and aeroplanes were eventually beaten. This was the decisive battle of the war. Many of the most prominent Welsh miner volunteers were killed. These included Harry Dobson of Blaenclydach, Sid James of Treherbert, Tom Howell Jones of Aberdare as well as the Llanelli steelworker Brazell Thomas.

One Catalonian lady addressed the men and women of the International Brigade as, 'You are history. You are legend. You are the heroic example of the solidarity and universality of democracy. We shall not forget you. And when the olive tree of peace puts forth its leaves, entwined with the laurels of the Spanish Republic's victory, come back, come back to us and you will find a homeland.'

And now that the last Welsh International Brigader has died, it is particularly important not to forget their deeds, and more importantly, what they were fighting for. Fascism was not wiped out by the victory of the 2nd World War.

In Spain, it lived on under the reign of Franco for another 30 years. Still today there are elements of Fascism in our society, and Wales and the Welsh, especially those from the Valleys, still identify with the great forces of liberty and democracy.

Wales and the Spanish Civil War: the Dragon's Dearest Cause. Robert Stradling, University of Wales Press, 2004

From Aberdare to Albacete, Edwin Greening. Warren & Pell, Wales, 2006

Wise and Foolish Dreamers. Phil Cope, Welsh Centre for International Affairs, 2007

Tasker Watkins VC

THE WELSH IN THE SECOND WORLD WAR

The 53rd Welsh Division fought in the 1st World War at Gallipoli, and against the Turks in Palestine. At the outbreak of the 2nd World war they went from Wales to garrison Ulster. After four years of training, they landed in Normandy as part of Overlord, one of Monty's six (green) divisions, but the only Welsh division. They took part in the attritional battles of Le Cahier, Le Bon Riposte and Evrecy.

It was during this time that Lt Tasker Watkins of the 1\5th Welsh Regiment won his VC. Born in Nelson, Glamorgan and educated at Pontypridd Grammar School, he was involved when the Welsh Regiment attacked objectives near Barfour. His company came under murderous machine gun fire while advancing through corn fields set with booby traps. At the head of his men, Lt Watkins now the only officer left, charged two machine gun posts, personally accounting for the occupants with his Sten gun.

Later, his gun jamming, he threw it in the face of a German anti- tank gunner, killing him at the same moment with a pistol shot. His small remnant counter attacked, Lt Watkins led a bayonet charge, destroying the enemy and finally at dusk, their wireless gone and separated from the battalion which had withdrawn, he ordered his men to scatter and himself personally charging and silencing an enemy machine gun post, he brought them back safely.

This officer's superb leadership not only saved his men's lives but decisively influenced the course of the battle. He was decorated with a V.C. by His Majesty King George VI at Buckingham Palace on 8th March, 1945. The 53rd Division, captured 4,000 Germans in the Falaise Gap before following up to Antwerp and the Lommel bridgehead Battles.

Their greatest set piece victory was the capture of Hertogenbosh in October 1944. Lt Gen Ritchie their corps commander wrote that he was tremendously impressed with the fighting qualities of the division. After a short spell as garrison of the 'island' they were abruptly called south as part of Monty's 'long stop' to fight the Panzers in the Ardennes in bitter conditions.

During 'Operation Veritable', they slogged their way through the Reichswale to break the Siegfried Line and into the Rhineland to capture Weeze. During Operation Plunder they fought in all the vicious little canal and river battles before ending the war in Hamburg. They suffered 10,000 casualties during the campaign; later Monty told them, 'You have been and are one of my best divisions.'

Now moving to the Far East, we look at Slim's Welsh general Major General Peter Rees in the Burma Campaign. He was born in Barry in 1898, the son of the Rev T M Rees. This place of birth stayed with him as he was known as 'The Docker' to the Welsh troops.

He was also known to the British troops as 'The Pocket Napoleon', a reference to his size and his success in battle. Slim said what he lacked in inches he made up for by the miles he advanced. Whether he was hallooing his troops from the roadside or leading them in his jeep, he was an inspiring divisional commander. The only criticism Slim made was to point out to him that the best huntsman did not invariably run ahead of the hounds.

His early military career included service with the 125th Napiers Rifles in Mesopotamia and Palestine during the 1st World War where he was awarded the D S O and the Military Cross.

In the 1920s and the 1930s, like most Indian army officers, he saw service on the North West Frontier and went on to serve as an instructor at the Royal Military Academy, Sandhurst. On the outbreak of the 2nd World War, Rees was commander of the 3rd Battalion the 6th RajPutana Rifles.

The Indian Army was the largest volunteer arm; two and a half million personnel served. Major General Henry 'Taffy' Davies, another Welshman who commanded 25th Indian Division in Burma commented in his memoir, 'The Division, as all soldiers know, is the basic fighting formation in practically any army in the world. It is large and powerful enough, with its establishment of about 17,000 men to have a decisive influence in any military operation. At the same time, it is sufficiently compact to enable its commander to exercise a personal leadership and control and to permit its functioning as a well co-ordinated team.

In the British Army during two World Wars, the divisional spirit has been something which has been fostered and nourished as an important matter of principle. It is interesting that, on the Burma front too, Lieutenant General Sir Jeffrey Evans and Brigadier Lloyd of the 5th Indian Infantry Brigade were also probably Welshmen.

From March 1941 Rees took command of 10th Brigade of the 5th Indian Division which fought in the Battle of Keren. By March 1942, he had taken over command of the 10th Indian Division. There was a blip in his career when he was relieved of his command over a misunderstanding of his defence of Sollum.

A debate went on about how suitable General Rees was to command a division, but after a short time with General Auchinleck, he went on to command 19th Indian Division.

General Slim and the changes he instituted, especially in the way troops were trained to fight in the jungle, helped to reverse the fortunes of the British against the Japanese. Rees, commenting on the jungle in a lecture, said, 'With regard to the jungle itself it is chiefly a matter of getting used to it and having the necessary equipment, which we now have, hacking knives etc. and even green coloured underwear and towels, green so that we can wash it and hang it out to dry without the fear of Japanese aircraft spotting it which would happen with white clothes against the jungle green background.'

In the attack in Burma, Rees drove the division straight for Mandalay down the Irrawaddy with the Shan mountains to the east taking Tongyi and Madaya on the way. Taung-in was captured by the 2nd Battalion the Welch Regiment on St David's Day.

In the regimental journal 'Men of Harlech' it said, 'We had no support for this advance except for our own mortars. During the advance we passed through a field of spring onions and many of the men wore them in their hats instead of leeks. We captured our objective late that evening at a cost of three wounded. The General arrived in our perimeter just before dark and wished us 'Dewi Sant'.'

Major General Pete Rees was an inspirational divisional commander who John Hill who served in 19th Indian Division commented that as a divisional commander, his reputation for leading from the front was no mere newspaper correspondent's exuberance or rumour.

It probably explains why like Slim, he was regarded by all of us Indians, Ghurkas and Britons alike as a soldier's general. He shared our battle experiences and talked our language whether Urdu, Gurkhali, Hindi or his native Welsh. He commanded the 19th Indian Division until the end of the 2nd World War, retiring from the Indian Army in 1948 and died in 1959.

It was Rees who said, 'Without boastfulness and acknowledging Divine Blessing, 14th Army may indeed be proud of its achievements, its comradeship between all races and creeds and its terrific fighting morale.'

To conclude, as in the 1st World War, the Welsh made a huge contribution in the 2nd with their generals, their fighting men and their courageous fighting spirit.

VCs of Wales and the Welsh Regiments. Alister Williams, Bridge Books, 1984

Heart of a Dragon, The Vcs of Wales and the Welsh Regiments. Bridge Books, 2006

Transactions of the Honourable Society of Cymmrodorion, Vol 12, p 147,2006

THE WELSH IN THE RAF

It is said that the Welsh do 'punch above their weight' in the armed forces, as they do contribute about 9% of the personnel. This is a greater proportion than their numbers in the United Kingdom and is also reflected in their contribution to the RAF. The author could not leave these out, as one of his great friends, Pilot Officer Mike Chappell would never let him forget it. Mike has done so much for the RAF Association in Wales, and should be highly commended for this.

We start off with Wing Commander Ken Rees who was involved in the Great Escape.

Wing Commander Ken Rees

From his obituary:

Ken Rees was piloting a Wellington bomber in a mine-laying operation in Norway in October of 1942 when it was shot down. He was able to crash land the aircraft in a lake and clamber up to the shore along with two other crew members; the other two who were with them lost their lives. Though they were saved from getting toasted or drowned, they were, nevertheless, captured by the enemy.

After going through an interrogation, Ken Rees was sent to Stalag Luft III, the prison camp for captured Allied airmen. While in prison, Ken Rees became the 'headache' of his captors. He was so troublesome and was fond of needling the prison guards that he was a regular guest of the 'cooler' — Stalag Luft's punishment block.

The antagonism Ken Rees showed towards the German guards of the prison camp stemmed from his anger when he learned that his brother-in-law – a pilot like himself – was machine-gunned by a German war plane.

Reportedly, Rees's brother-in-law had bailed out of his burning Hurricane and was floating earthward when the German craft did the deed. As Ken Rees recounted in his later years, he, along with the others, had vowed to agitate the Germans as they felt almost invincible, so capable and well-trained.

When the time came that Squadron Leader Roger Bushell, the escape committee's head (known as the Big X), contrived the plans for the mass breakout from Stalag Luft III, Ken Rees was chosen to be part of the digging team. Later on, the WWII veteran admitted that he might have been chosen on the basis that he was a Welshman and might have had some experience in mining which was not really the case.

The escape plan required the clandestine digging of three tunnels – nicknamed Tom, Dick and Harry – with the third being the longest. Harry was planned to stretch out for as long as 330 feet with its end resting in some woods beyond Stalag Luft's perimeter wire. Nothing like it was planned before. Eventually, Tom was discovered and Dick abandoned.

Ken Rees then devoted his digging time for the realization of Harry. The flight lieutenant was a stocky and powerfully built man. His digging time provided him with the distraction he needed from the boredom and the hunger he was constantly feeling in prison. It got him through one of last century's coldest winters.

The risk of the tunnel collapsing and burying them under soft sand was constantly hovering over the diggers. Throughout the digging, they experienced several roof falls which they had to correct using the boards of their prison beds.

Finally, after digging out 250 tons of sand, their great escape was set for the night between the 24th and 25th of March,1944. The entrance to Harry was hidden in Hut 104 and all 200 men involved in the plan were gathered there at the appointed time before the guards shut down the huts. They had their escape kits with them.

Ken Rees described that night as stomach-churning, the feeling much worse than what he felt as he waited for a bombing campaign to start. Seeing a German officer among the men in the hut, he was alarmed, though he discovered later on that it was just a fellow prisoner in a sophisticated disguise. That night, they executed their plan. However, when the diggers broke out of the surface, they realized that their tunnel did not quite reach the woods they were aiming for. This slowed down their progress causing delays.

Eventually, 76 men were able to clamber out onto the surface while Ken Rees was crouching low in the tunnel, guiding them. His time to leave came and he was almost at the exit ladder when a shot was fired. That was the signal that the escape had been discovered. In a rush and on all fours, Ken Rees made his way through the tunnel back to the hut and was the last to clamber up before the tunnel's trap door was closed. When he got in, he found the other prisoners, burning their forged papers and eating the emergency rations. Only moments after the frenzy, German forces arrived.

Ken Rees was promptly sent to the 'cooler'. There, he heard that 50 of his colleagues were shot by the Gestapo. Along with these 50 men were Roger Bushell and his great friend Johnny Bull. Ken Rees later pointed out that he would have been one of the 50 men executed had he got out that fateful night. After all, he was a 'hot sight' for the Germans given the regular visits he had to the 'cooler' and his antagonistic attitude towards the German guards of the prison.

Another escape tunnel was planned later that year, but the fear of getting discovered and shot as well as the fast progress the Allies were making against the Germans led to the abandonment of the plan. Late January of 1945 rolled in.

It was this time that Ken Rees and the other Stalag Luft prisoners were told to collect their scanty belongings at an hour's notice and leave the camp. The Soviets were advancing to the east as the Germans made their escape, bringing the prisoners with them. Suffering from severe hardships mixed with bitter cold weather, the guards commanded Rees and the other prisoners to advance westward.

After more than three gruesome months, on May 2 that same year, Ken Rees and the other Stalag Luft prisoners were liberated by the advancing British troops. In no time, Rees was headed to the safety of his home and to his wife, whom he had married just days before he was shot down.

When the WWII veteran was told that Steve McQueens's character in the 1963 American war film *The Great Escape* was based on him, he stated that he had nothing to do with that story. He further added that McQueen was a 6-foot tall American while he was a short and stocky Welshman. Apart from that, he did not know how to ride a motorbike. He eventually pointed out that the only similarities he could see between himself and Captain Hilts, McQueen's character, were that they always annoyed the Germans and were constant visitors of the 'cooler'.

Air Marshall Sir Ivor Broom

He was a lad from the Rhondda Valley who rose from the rank of Sergeant Pilot to Air Marshall, being awarded on the way the DSO, 3 DFCs and an AFC. He completed three tours of operations over enemy territory, including

31 extremely dangerous low level attacks on enemy targets from the beleaguered island of Malta.

In 1955, he set a new speed record flying from Canada to England in a Canberra bomber, became commandant of CFS which included the management and operation control of the Red Arrows, and commanded the strategically important No 11 Group during the period of The Cold War. In 1974 he took over as deputy controller of the National Air Traffic Services and retired from the RAF in 1977.

Squadron Leader Hughie Idwal Edwards

He was born in Western Australia of Welsh parents, and was one of the bravest men in the Royal Air Force in the Second World War. His citation for the VC on 4th July, 1941 was based on his leadership of an important attack on the Port of Bremen, one of the most heavily defended towns in Germany. Although he was handicapped by a physical disability arising from a flying accident, he pressed home bombing attacks from very low heights.

On reaching Bremen, flying at a height of little more than 50 feet, he was met with a hail of fire, all his aircraft being hit and four of them destroyed. Nevertheless, he made a most successful attack and then, with the greatest skill and coolness, withdrew the surviving aircraft without further loss.

Already, on 1st July 1941, he had led a formation of aircraft on an operational sweep against enemy shipping off the Dutch coast. In the face of intense and accurate machine gun fire, the formation attacked from a height of only 50 feet. His citation for the DFC said that, at all times, he had displayed great leadership, skill and gallantry.

Flight Lieutenant David Lord

He came from Wrexham, and was given a citation for a VC on 13th November, 1945. While flying at 1,500 feet over the Battle of Arnhem, the starboard wing of his aircraft was twice hit by anti-aircraft fire. He would have been justified in leaving the mainstream of supplying aircraft but, realising that his crew were uninjured and the troops would be in dire need of supplies, he completed his mission. His task finished, Flt-Lt Lord ordered the crew to abandon the Dakota, making no attempt himself to leave the aircraft which was down to 500 feet. A few seconds later, the starboard wing collapsed and the aircraft fell in flames. There was only one survivor. By remaining at the controls to give his crew a chance to escape, Flt-Lt Lord displayed supreme valour and self-sacrifice.

The V.C.s of Wales and the Welsh Regiments. W Alister Williams, Bridge Books, Wales, 1984

Clean Sweep. Tony Broomer, Crécy Books Ltd, 1984

Major Alun Harrhy

THE ROYAL REGIMENT OF WALES IN IRELAND 1972

1972 was by far the worst year of the troubles, and never again will the deaths of soldiers, terrorists or the incidence of bombings and shootings ever reach these heights again. It would witness 1,853 bombings, 10,564 shootings and the deaths of 129 soldiers, 17 RUC officers, 223 civilians and 98 terrorists.

This year would see the appalling 'Bloody Friday' attacks when the IRA planted bombs in Belfast's bus depot. It would also witness the awful slaughter at the Abercorn restaurant in Donegal Street in Belfast which killed four civilians, 'Operation Motorman' was carried out by British Army forces with the operation starting at 4am on 31st July to retake the no-go areas (i.e. areas controlled by the Provisional IRA) established in Belfast and Derry in the aftermath of internment the previous year.

The operation used 27 infantry and three armoured battalions aided by 5,300 UDR men. The IRA did not attempt to hold their ground as they lacked the necessary armaments and numbers for a direct confrontation with the army.

The British Army employed an overwhelming force of 22,000 troops, roughly 4 per cent of the British Army. By the end of the day there were no more no-go areas in Ireland.

The Royal Regiment of Wales moved into the Ardoyne and Shankhill area in April 1972; their tour was conducted with a backdrop of constant gun battles and the radio air waves were clogged up by the shouts of, 'Contact-wait-out'.

During that time, the battalion lost six men, all killed within a period of just two months. In addition to Private John Hillman, and Lance Corporal Peter Heppenstall, the RRW lost four more men in what was the worst period for them in the whole Northern Ireland campaign.

On June 12th, Private Alan Giles died of his wounds having been shot the previous day in a gun battle in Alliance Avenue on the Ardoyne. Just 7 days later, Private Brian Soden who was 21 and married with two children was shot in the head and fatally wounded in the Ardoyne by an IRA gunman using armour piercing rounds. And then in a terrible two day period for the Welsh lads, on July 13th, Pte David Meeke was shot and killed at Hooker Street and on the next day Heppenstall was killed and Pte John Williams was shot and killed on Alliance Avenue, having been lured into an ambush by an explosion.

The RRW's difficulties had been added to by the emergence of the more militant Protestants who under the organisation of the Ulster Defence Association had started to make their own no-go areas in Belfast.

On Sunday 21st May, the regiment were presented with a tricky problem when the Protestants cut the famous Shankhill Road in three places with hijacked lorries, buses and cars. The regiment were prepared to take these barricades down, which would have created huge problems with the Protestants but the latter did agree to remove the barricades.

The Protestants, too, had been on a rampage of violence, especially in the Bone Hill area. 'A' Company was involved in a tragic incident when the IRA gunned down a young girl near the company base. The Protestants suspected the Welsh of being slightly tainted by Nationalism and therefore slightly sympathetic towards the Catholics.

There is no doubt that, as counter insurgency troops in such situations as these, the Welsh boys with their good humour and slightly relaxed confidence were excellent at damping down hugely awkward situations.

'A' Company were in constant battle with rioting youths, and, on two nights, employed the Neptune water cannon. This was a success to start with, but the youths, soaking wet on hot nights, quite enjoyed the soaking.

The author was engaged in patrols in the Bone area, where often in the alleyways dog muck with glass was spread by the IRA so the soldiers would get it on their boots and the sound would give them away. Also there were a number of hits recorded against the IRA but often the bodies were hidden and stuffed down the sewers and disappeared so the military could not record a hit.

The worst part of the area in many ways was the Ardoyne and the adjoining link with the Bone, a particularly unpleasant enclave, ripe in IRA activity.

The author spent some time in a ruined factory overlooking the path from the Ardoyne to the Bone with another sniper, prepared to take out movements of arms between the two areas. We all knew we were in Northern Ireland to try and prevent all- out war breaking out between the Catholics and Protestants.

Our job was a very difficult one, especially as we had to take on both sides although the Protestants were perhaps slightly more amenable with their cups of tea and biscuits. There was no doubt that the soldiers felt slightly safer in Protestant areas, which inevitably meant that they warmed more to the Protestant side.

The atmosphere was one of hatred and insecurity despite some appearances of normality; the soldiers could never rely on the absence of threats to their security.

In many ways it was a huge waiting game; the initiative was held by the gunmen who waited for patrols, taking quick and sometimes accurate shots at the leading men before disappearing.

At the end of three months, the author himself knew that he was reaching the end of his tether and luckily for him, before the end of the tour, he was sent off on a training course to Warminster.

Major John Ayres

The author would like to pay tribute to his 'A' Company commander, Major John Ayres, who, with his bulldog spirit and great sense of fairness and courage, maintained morale and order in a beleaguered 'A' Company: his leadership was outstanding and he was helped by his very cool and reassuring Captain Andy Keelan, his second in command.

The bravery of his fellow platoon commanders, NCOs and soldiers in a dire situation was also commendable. The nerves were frayed even more by the positions of the company bases which were often right in the middle of the action- no one was safe. On one occasion, in 'A' Company, a man was sent out to clean the company area but, in the process, was shot.

Northern Ireland is an integral part of the United Kingdom; a majority of the people are Protestant but the high-handed way in which their power brokers dealt with the Catholics who felt down trodden and abused created the enormous friction which led to the troubles. There is no doubt that the IRA's campaign was effective in bringing the British government to the peace table, and eventually led to power sharing.

The troubles lie deep in history, much of which was caused by the brutality of the British government. The Welsh were deeply implicated, as Elizabeth Tudor put many Scots settlers into Northern Ireland.

Oliver Cromwell's real name was Oliver Morgan Williams and Lloyd George sent in the 'Black and Tans'. It was not only the Anglo Irish or English landlords that drove the Irish off the land, but there were also Welsh families like the Vaughans and the Herberts who were involved.

Ireland has been a running sore for the United Kingdom, and some Welsh Nationalists would say that at least the South had the guts to go independent. There is no democratic will in Wales to go the same way. The Welsh are an integral part of the United Kingdom, and many of them over the years have been at the centre of power broking.

After Oliver Cromwell né Williams, there were three Prime Ministers of Welsh stock; Lord Salisbury, Lloyd George and Mrs Thatcher whose father, Alderman Roberts's family, were of Welsh stock. It is a great sadness that the troubles included the death of Airey Neave, blown up by the IRA in the House of Commons carpark. The author's father gave him the Anglican equivalent of last rites when he was badly wounded at the Battle of Calais, and they became friends.

The troubles still simmer but the Peace Agreement was a triumph, and in the Welsh context, the author's friend and mentor, Lord Paul Murphy, a Welshman of Irish roots was a leading architect under Mo Mowlam.

The Royal Regiment of Wales has now disappeared as an entity; some would say that the amalgamation of the South Wales Borderers and the Welch Regiment was not a great success, but we are now in a melting pot with the Royal Welsh Fusiliers called the Royal Welsh which allows us a united front as the only Welsh regiment of the line without Darwinian competition undermining the unity and team spirit. It is important that Wales, as it always has done, makes a significant contribution to the defence of our realm.

Major Alun Harrhy is one of the great stalwarts of the branches, and an incredibly brave man, having sustained awful injuries while training. I salute him as one of the examples of the great Welsh soldiers of the modern day.

A Long Long War. Ken Wharton, Helion & Company, 2008

A History of the Royal Regiment of Wales. J M Brereton, Regimental Headquarters, The Royal Regiment of Wales (24th/41st Foot) Cardiff, 1989

Bullets, Bombs and Cups of Tea. Ken Wharton, Helion & Company Ltd, 2009

Also Authors own experiences in Northern Ireland 1972

Lord Herbert of Cherbury
Founder of the Royal Welch Fusiliers

THE ROYAL WELCH FUSILIERS IN BOSNIA

By Colonel Nick Lock OBE

With the death of the leader of Yugoslavia, Marshal Tito in 1980 and the end of the Cold War following the fall of the Berlin Wall, the country of Yugoslavia rapidly descended into civil war. Europe had not seen such levels of ethnic violence since the end of the Second World War.

A number of small, international, observer missions were deployed to the region but this did little to stem the tide of a vicious inter-ethnic conflict. Public and press opinion in Great Britain finally led, in September 1992, to the deployment of HQ 11 Armoured Brigade and 1st Battalion the Cheshire Regiment, an Armoured Infantry Battlegroup, equipped with Warrior armoured vehicles.

The first British soldier to be killed in Bosnia was a Royal Welch Fusilier, Lance Corporal Wayne Edwards, who had been attached to the Cheshire's Battlegroup. British Forces were deployed under a United Nations Security Council Resolution as part of the UN Protection Force (UNPROFOR). UNPROFOR's mandate under which the force operated was limited to Peacekeeping rather than Peace Enforcement (using force to impose a peace).

The British contribution to the mission continued to expand through 1993-94 by which time there was a full brigade of troops, including armoured infantry and mechanised infantry battlegroups, an armoured reconnaissance regiment, engineer regiment and supporting logistics troops. The force was distributed through central Bosnia Hercegovina, with the majority of the mechanised battlegroup deployed to the eastern enclave of Goražde, with D Company detached in central Bosnia and a logistic hub in the port of Split on the Croatian coast.

The 1st Battalion, The Royal Welch Fusiliers, (1RWF) had recently moved from a mechanised infantry role in 1 Mechanized Brigade, based in Tidworth, Wiltshire, to a light role infantry battal-ion based at RAF Brawdy near Haverford West, in West Wales.

At this time, there was no plan for the battalion to deploy on an operational tour to Bosnia. This changed however with the recognition that operations in Bosnia could extend for some time and that 1 RWF with recent mechanised experience on the Saxon armoured vehicle should be utilised before this experience dissipated.

The Commanding Officer Lt Col J.P. Riley, Operations Officer Capt N.J. Lock and Quartermaster Maj A. Redburn deployed on a reconnaissance in November 1994. This reconnaissance provided a taste of what was to come with a difficult winter journey into Goražde by road (no helicopters were allowed into the enclaves by the BSA). The Goražde enclave was one of three UN sanctioned "Safe Areas" in Eastern Bosnia along with Zĕpa with Ukrainian UNPROFOR and Srebrenica with Dutch UNPROFOR troops.

The status of these Safe Areas was never fully defined or agreed but in late 1994 a Cessation of Hostilities Agreement (COHA) was in place. These three enclaves contained significant numbers of the Bosnian Muslim civilians and troops. They were isolated and surrounded by the Bosnian Serb Army (BSA) who controlled all movement into the enclaves including that of UNPROFOR troops.

The journey from the A2 Echelon established at Kiseljak, in Bosnian Croatian territory, into Sarajevo and on to Goražde was slow going requiring passage through numerous BSA checkpoints. UNPROFOR convoys to Goražde where subject to BSA authorisation and constant harassment on the route. In the light of recent operations in Iraq and Afghanistan, operating under such restrictions in Bosnia seems incredible.

In the early 1990s however, the UNPROFOR mandate was not robust enough to allow complete freedom of movement and robust reactions to ceasefire violations.

Against this backdrop, 1 RWF deployed as a battlegroup to Bosnia in February 1995. Goražde Force, as the composite force was titled, consisted of 1 RWF (less D Company who were deployed to Bugojno in central Bosnia), a Ukrainian mechanised company, a Norwegian surgical team (NORMED) and a UN Military Observer (UNMO) team.

No-one in the battalion was under any illusions that this promised to be a challenging six-month tour but events would unfold that would see intensity of sustained combat not seen by the British Army since the Korean War.

The RWF conducted a relief-in-place in late February 1995 with the 1st Battalion, The Royal Gloucestershire, Berkshire, and Wiltshire (RGBW) Regiment. 1 RGBW had lost a number of soldiers through Saxon armoured vehicles falling off the treacherous mountain roads and tracks demonstrating the terrain was just as dangerous as the warring factions in the Goražde area.

1 RWF took command of the UN operations in the Goražde Safe Area on the 1st of March 1995, St David's Day being celebrated by all ranks in the battalion. The town of Goražde was bisected by the River Drina which acted as the inter-company boundary between A Company north of the river and B Company to the south (see Map 2) with C Company being responsible for the area to the south west.

The main base for the battalion was in the old bus station and athletics field will within the town. The troops then occupied fourteen observation posts (OPs) on the high ground above the town.

These OPs were co-located in many places with BSA positions as the Serbs occupied the all the high ground enabling them to fire into Goražde at will. And so it was that the RWF inherited a force lay down that was militarily defendable but provided the only area in theatre where UNPROFOR were actively patrolling the confrontation lines.

On arrival Agreement between the factions on the status of Goražde had placed a 3 Kilometre Total Exclusion Zone (TEZ) around the town in which the BSA [deleted] could not openly carry weapons. The ceasefire known as the COHA, brokered by ex-President Jimmy Carter,was due to run out at the end of April and with no prospect of a renewal all were aware of the fragility situation.

The Fusiliers settled into a routine of liaison, patrolling and where appropriate enforcing the TEZ restrictions. Their mandate and rules of engagement were far from ideal, only able to respond with force if directly targeted. The OPs resembled First World War dugouts which would have made many previous generations of Royal Welchmen feel very much at home.

During the first three months of the tour patrols were established into all areas of the Safe Area and this was often dangerous work with RWF patrols coming under fire almost every other day. These gun battles could range from a few shots often fired by drug-crazed combatants to sustained ambushes.

One such event took place in the village of Podkevacev Dol, when an A Company patrol, lead by Lt Hugh Nightingale, having entered an abandoned house came under sustained fire from 40mm Bofors Anti-Aircraft guns. These guns were fired in the direct fire role and literally started to demolish the house in which the Fusiliers had taken cover. The patrol gave as good as it got returning over 700 rounds at the BSA positions. Lt Nightingale was later awarded the Military Cross for his outstanding leadership.

In another incident, a patrol from B Company, found themselves in the middle of a BiH minefield. The lead

Fusilier stood on an improvised mine, which detonated, wounding him in the face.

The rest of the patrol believing he had been shot, dashed forward to assist, whereupon two more soldiers stood on mines becoming casualties. Corporal Williams 49, the last remaining man in the patrol, who had only arrived in the enclave that day, showed great courage and with the help of some BiH soldiers, went forward and retrieved the casualties. These three men were the only casualties to be evacuated from Goražde by helicopter. Cpl Williams 49 was Mentioned in Dispatches for his actions.

Where possible, under the UN Rules of Engagement, the Royal Welshmen did their best to pro-tect civilian life.

In one incident, a small Bosnian Muslim school, in the village of Vitkovici which was on the confrontation line, was being sniped at by BSA forces with medium and heavy ma-chine guns. By inter-positioning a number of their Saxons the Fusiliers were able to act robustly to BSA snipers, returning over 600 rounds and silencing a number of BSA positions.

The COHA ended on the 1st May and with it, a new, much more dangerous period of operations rapidly developed. It was clear that with no formal ceasefire in place there would be very little peace to keep for the UNPROFOR troops. As freedom of movement for UNPROFOR became much more restricted, Goražde Force received increasingly less frequent resupply convoys. Contingency plans were put in place with minimal vehicle movement, cooking and heating all water on wood fires to save fuel. Eventually, food also needed to be rationed and the lack of fresh food over time, had a significant impact on the health of many Fusiliers.

As the month of May progressed, the situation deteriorated with BiH attacks in the vicinity of Sarajevo heightened tensions across Bosnia. BSA forces began to move heavy weapons into exclusion zones and engage the Bosnian Muslim areas.

Gen Rupert Smith, the British General in command of UNPROFOR issued an ultimatum for BSA heavy weapons to be removed which Gen Mladic, the BSA commander, refused to do. With UNPROFOR's credibility at stake, Gen Smith ordered air strikes on BSA positions on the 24th and 25th of May. In response, the BSA started shelling across Bosnia.

It was clear that the current Goražde Force Camp, within the town of Goražde and the exposed OP line were extremely vulnerable to BSA shelling and direct attacks. During the night of the 25th May, manning of the OP line and main camp were thinned out and with the exception of a security force and tactical headquarters, the remainder of Goražde Force conducted a highly successful extraction to an area outside the town and out of BSA direct fire weapons range. Contingency plans were enacted and the Royal Welch, with the use of the code word "Dragon's Teeth" conducted all their radio communications in Welsh for added security.

The 26th and 27th May were relatively quiet but on the 28th May three OPs in A Company's area, on the Sjenokos Mountain, were rapidly surrounded and significantly outnumbered by heavily armed BSA troops. With no ability to initiate a standoff and with restrictive rules of engagement, the OP commanders were forced to surrender their OPs rather than risk a massacre. As the Royal Welchmen were moved away from the confrontation line, one of their Saxons rolled off the mountain road and down a steep hillside. There were a number of significant injuries but no deaths. Elsewhere in the enclave it was now clear what was going on and Goražde Force was put on high alert. In B Company's area large numbers of BSA troops were also manoeuvring and one of B Company's OPs also were surrounded.

Now on full alert Royal Welch OPs began a desperate fight for survival as heavy firefights broke out all across the mountains dominating Goražde. BiH forces were now aware of the danger posed by the BSA offensive and rapid streamed out of the town with the aim of getting to the Goražde Force ops before the BSA did. If the Serbs captured these positions then they could fire directly into the town at will. What was required was for the OPs to destroy any useful equipment in location and then withdraw in good order.

Over the next three hours the remaining A and B Company troops fought a skilled and well-rehearsed fighting withdrawal. Major Richard Westley, commanding B Company would receive a Military Cross for his outstanding leadership south of the River Drina in extracting his Company.

One of the most remote OPs in the B Company area was commanded by CSgt Pete Humphries. Humphries quickly realised that his position was surrounded. Keeping half his force in their hill top OP to give covering fire, he sent the other half in a Saxon down the mountain heading back into Goražde. With Serb heavy machine gun fire bouncing of the vehicle and supported with fire from Humphries's team, the Saxon smashed through a BSA roadblock to escape into Goražde. Humphries then lead the rest of his team, on foot down an emergency escape route.

On route, he encountered three groups of Serbs, each time he caught them by surprise and faced them down having pulled the pins on live hand grenades. He then personally led his team through a minefield to get them safely into Goražde. For his actions, CSgt Humphries was awarded the second Conspicuous Gallantry Cross ever awarded.

There were numerous other acts of bravery and courage across Goražde Force that day. At the conclusion of the day, the battalion had thirty-three men held hostage by the Serbs but the remainder of the force had been safely extracted from the OP line where the BiH now had a foot hold preventing the complete domination of Goražde by the Serbs.

With the COHA comprehensively compromised, there was no peace left for UNPROFOR to keep. The town and the Goražde Force base came under heavy shelling with over a thousand artillery shells landing in and around the town on many of the following days.

The Royal Welchmen stayed under cover during the day but there were a good number of near misses.

Fighting continued through June but a relative stalemate developed so that by the 21st June a lull in the fighting allowed troops to move out of their battle positions and establish a more normal routine. Shortly afterwards, a UN convoy finally made it into the enclave after a period of six weeks with no resupply. This was essential as the force had been on half rations for two weeks and had just three days food left.

This convoy helped to re-establish some semblance of freedom of movement and some troops finally moved out of the enclave on R&R but would not return. It was now clear that the UN forces in the enclaves were not present in sufficient strength to de-fend them and were potentially preventing the UN's freedom to take action as they were vulnerable to be taken hostage.

This thinning out of troops was well in hand when the Serbs attacked Srebrenica and then Žepa. This was a clear turning point in the campaign and the UN and NATO issued the Serbs with an ultimatum. In Goražde, the BiH now became much more hostile to UN forces in the aftermath of Srebrenica. They attacked the Ukrainian Company, based in an old factory to the south of Goražde town and disarmed them. A few days later, elements on the BiH attacked the Royal Welch's camp. A large firefight ensued which resulted in a number of BiH soldiers killed but no injuries to Royal Welchmen.

It was clear to Gen Smith, the UNPROFOR Commander, that Goražde Force would need to be withdrawn before NATO could commence any air attacks against the Serbs.

Following the shelling of crowed Sarajevo market by the Serbs on the 28th August more air strikes were likely to be authorised. At very short notice, the remaining elements of 1 RWF were ordered out of Goražde and in a very swift move that caught booth the BSA and BiH by surprise the remaining troops formed up in a convoy of vehicles and effectively crashed through the confrontation line and conducted a rapid road move to the Serbian border before either side could react to stop the convoy.

So concluded one of the most extraordinary operational tours conducted by British troops since the Second World War. When confronted with a savage civil war on its doorstep the European nations and the UN had learnt some tough lessons about the use of lightly armed forces for Peacekeeping when what was required was a Peace Enforcement mission. This had resulted in a British Infantry Battalion being inserted into an isolated outpost with little prospect of timely support.

Valuable lessons were learnt which meant that subsequent interventions such as that in Kosovo and Sierra Leone were made with sufficient force and the right authorities. Today, the Royal Welch Fusiliers story of many courageous Welshmen's actions is not that well known.

The battalion did however receive appropriate recognition with the largest number of operational awards being made to the battalion, for a single operational tour, since the Korean War. This very publicly recognised that in the words of the Regiment's Collect, this generation of Royal Welsh-men had indeed "Upheld the Ancient Valour of The Royal Welch Fusiliers".

Article by Colonel Nick Lock OBE, formerly operations officer in Bosnia

THE QUEEN'S DRAGOON GUARDS

This essay is unfortunately rather shallow in its content, partly because the curator in the Queen's Dragoon Guards Museum in Cardiff was handing over and did not have enough time to help me. (Ed)

They are known as the Welsh Cavalry as from about the 1960s they started to recruit from Wales. The author knows this because when he was in the Welsh Brigade depot in Crickhowell, two QDG officers served in the army youth team there on attachment.

They were both splendid officers for whom he had huge respect – David Walsh, a horseman and Peter Holdsworth, also a horseman and boxer. In addition to this, the author knew some other interesting officers, Chris Mackenzi-Beevor was with him in Sandhurst and became colonel of the regiment; Colonel Georgie Powell was the author's college commander at Sandhurst and Richard Parry a good friend. Also Quentin Braoul's mother was a Welsh lady whose parents were great friends of the author's father.

One of the author's friends at Sandhust was Iestyn Thomas, a great rugby player, who at the end of his first term at Sandhurst didn't want to join the infantry but wanted to join the cavalry. When he went to join the QDG one of the first questions he was asked was did he have a private income. He was so incensed that he left the army immediately. However, the author certainly doesn't believe this elitism still happens.

The current regiment was formed in 1959 by the amalgamation of the 1st Kings Dragoon Guards raised in 1685 as the 2nd Queen's Regiment of Horse by James II of England in reaction to the Monmouth Rebellion and the 2nd Dragoon Guards, the Queen's Bays.

The regiment has spent much of its history based in Germany, but has seen active service in Borneo, Aden, Lebanon, the 1991 Gulf War, Bosnia, Kosovo, Northern Ireland, the 2003 Iraq War and deployments to Afghanistan in 2008 and 2009, and 2011-2012.

In 1983 the regiment was deployed to Lebanon in support of the Allied Multi National Force. In 1990 it was sent to the Middle East for the Gulf War, and in 1996 it was deployed to Bosnia as part of NATO peacekeeping forces during the Yugoslav Wars.

In 2003, the regiment served in Iraq during the invasion of Iraq providing the reconnaissance light armour support necessary to allow 3 commander brigades advance north to Basra. Their main role was to spearhead the route north towards Basra to where troops could push on to Baghdad. The QDG were involved in stopping up to 50 Iraqi tanks moving south of the city of Basra when they joined with helicopter gunships and the Royal Marines in the operation.

In their two gruelling tours of Afghanistan they lost two men. On the last tour of Afghanistan, their commanding officer Lt Will Davies said the regiment will leave behind a much better place than they found. During the operations in and around Basra, members of the regiment were awarded for their efforts in destroying more than 20 Iraqi tanks by being presented with a commando dagger by the Royal Marines. It was thought to be the first time an army unit had received such recognition.

Perhaps the best known member in the 1970s was Captain Mark Phillips, one time husband of Princess Anne. There has been some research by Michael Rhodes into Mark Phillips's ancestry and it seems to take the Phillips family back to a John Phillips, lime burner of Treflach in Oswestry, Shropshire buried 26th June 1805 aged 79. It seems probable this was a Welsh family.

It is interesting that when the author met a rear admiral in Brecon with the former mayor of Brecon, the former said that the QDGs weren't fit for the role. This was after they completed their second tour of Afghanistan and the author was amused when he discovered the admiral had never been involved in action. As far as everybody was concerned, the QDGs had operated at the highest level of professionalism in all their tours.

The author has not been able to find specific examples of gallantry, but they obviously did occur during the tour's experience. There was huge speculation at one stage that the regiment would be got rid of or amalgamated; however, a huge fight by the people of Wales, in particular, ensured that the regiment was kept, although it has a much smaller number of troops than the average infantry regiment.

It now operates in a light cavalry role and is equipped with Jackal armoured fighting vehicles. The UK ceased all combat operations in Afghanistan and withdrew the last of its combat troops on the 27 October 2014.

In terms of the cavalry order of precedence, it is only preceded by the Blues and Royals, so it is a very senior cavalry regiment.

Simon Weston

THE WELSH IN THE FALKLANDS INCLUDING LT COL H JONES VC AND THE WELSH GUARDS IN AFGHANISTAN

There were some officers who asked in bewilderment what possessed the Ministry of Defence to send two public duties battalions to the South Atlantic. Both Guards battalions joined 5 Brigade from prolonged tours of ceremonial duties, during which their infantry training was obviously less intensive than that of a marine or parachute battalion. They were trained to fight from armoured personnel carriers, and of them their officers said, 'We are not Bergen soldiers'.

Many believed they were sent to serve as a garrison, not to have to fight. They were considered a reserve for 3 Commando Brigade, not a force to match their capabilities. Certainly one Special Forces soldier I met felt they were not as fit as they should have been. On the afternoon of 3 June, 1982, they attempted to march to Goose Green, walking for 12 hours before it was agreed the march should be abandoned.

The Guardsmen were far too heavily laden. 3 Commando Brigade believed the Guardsmen had failed to perform even a modest yomp over the hills, and also they lacked the priceless Volvo tracked vehicles that were so good for carrying equipment. After this, some of the Welsh Guards were moved to Bluff Cove.

The Prince of Wales Company, 3 Company and the mortar platoon and support echelon of the Welsh Guards had been transferred aboard the ship 'Galahad' to sail to Fitzroy. The Welsh Guards were under orders to join the rest of their battalion at Bluff Cove.

To the Guards who had boarded the LSL from the shore, their senior officer seemed determined that his men should not be mucked about any more after all their movements and counter movements of the last few days. Landing craft were brought out to the ship but, because the craft were half loaded with ammunition, the Welsh Guards officers refused to put the men and the ammunition in the same boats. The rest is history.

Two Mirages and Skyhawks attacked the 'Galahad'. A large consignment of petrol for Rapier generators was aboard 'Galahad'; this ignited immediately, inflicting terrible burns on scores of Welsh Guardsmen assembling to board the landing craft. The horror was compounded by the ignition of white phosphorus bombs carried by the mortar platoon.

Within seconds of the first bomb landing, the whole of the centre of the ship was burning furiously. Men saw their own skin and flesh fry and melt before their eyes, as if in slow motion. They watched others fighting to dowse flames in their hair and to rip off their own burning clothing.

With great courage, several officers and men fought their way through a tangle of wreckage to the lower decks to shut off machinery. Others launched the ship's boats.

Away from the Welsh Guards, in another sphere of the battle for the Falklands, Lt Col Herbert Jones was commanding 2 Para. His fascination with the business of war had always gone beyond professional duty. The son of a prosperous West Country land owning family and the brother of a naval officer, H joined the Devon and Dorset Regiment after Eton and transferred to the Paras in 1980.

At the age of 42, there was still a boyishness about him, a charm and devastating grin that could light up his face. His second in command said he was intolerant in some ways; he would not suffer fools but he had a habit of being right. He was a real leader.

The author occasionally drinks with his brother in Wales who says that although his father's father and grandfather emigrated from Pembrokeshire to the USA, his mother Olwen Jones was daughter of Mr Pritchard-Jones J P of Holyhead, Anglesey; H however never perceived himself as Welsh.

In the attack towards Darwin, H had pinpointed a machine gun that he believed he could take out. Clutching his Sterling sub machine gun, followed by Sgt Norman and Lance Corporal Beresford he began to dash up a gully towards it. Seconds later he was hit in the back of the neck by a bullet fired from higher up the hill behind him which plunged through his body; he fell mortally wounded.

Some suggested that his dash up Darwin hill was responsible, but his second in command Major Keeble pointed out that at the moment the Colonel made his move, 2 Para's essential problem was that it had lost the ability to manoeuvre tactically in the face of the overwhelming enemy fire. The vital task was to break the deadlock.

At that moment, H with his tactical headquarters team represented precious firing, fighting power on Darwin hill. He was determined to make use of it. He was simply doing what he wanted his battalion to do, in Keeble's words. His lonely charge was an act in the British Army's great tradition of battalion leadership on the battlefield. He became a national hero.

Thereafter, the momentum of the attack was rapidly regained, Darwin and Goose Green were liberated and the battalion released the local inhabitants unharmed and forced the surrender of some 1,200 of the enemy. The achievements of 2nd battalion the Parachute Regiment at Darwin and Goose Green set the tone for the subsequent land victory on the Falklands.

H's action was the utmost gallantry by a commanding officer whose dashing leadership and courage throughout the battle were an inspiration to all about him.

There is no doubt that in Afghanistan, the Welsh Guards destroyed any stigma that might have become attached to them in the Falklands. In the offensive of summer 2009, their battlegroup advanced into the Helmand river valley.

At the beginning of the advance they achieved total surprise by driving into the heart of the main town of Basharan. The Prince of Wales company moved up to Chah-eAngir known as the Prize in the North. The Taliban counter attacked time and again.

At one stage Sgt Parry 700 and his men were holding the eastern position of the town with no cover other than ditches in the fields. This bold and daring move allowed no 2 company to proceed through them as they moved north in a mixture of Mastiffe, Ridgeback and Viking vehicles.

The commanding officer, realising how hard pressed his men were, was determined to get up to the front. He rode in the lead vehicle, occupying the top cover position and taking a full part in the operation to check the road ahead. There was a massive explosion and the commanding officer was killed. He was only the second Welsh Guards officer to be killed in action in Afghanistan.

When the battalion returned to the UK, despite the casualties, the reality was that their battle group had laid the foundations for securing the operational area. The regiment had acquitted itself with great bravery and professionalism in Afghanistan.

Bearskins, Bayonets & Body Armour. Trevor Royle, Frontline Books, 2015

Dead Men Risen. Toby Harnden, Quercus, 2011,

The Battle for the Falklands. Max Hastings & Simon Jenkins, Pan Books Ltd, 1983

Epilogue

The Welsh have been slightly neglected in their contribution to the British Empire, but nevertheless it has been a profound one. As a result of the poverty many of the Celts lived in, their territories were great hunting grounds for the recruiters of soldiers and sailors, and as such, have proved their courage time and time again in the battles of the British Empire in particular.

The Welsh were integral to the founding of the British Empire with the Tudors involvement, and to the establishment of the modern British parliamentary state through the winning of the Civil war by Cromwell and the American state with the Declaration of American Independence written by Jefferson.

In a time when sport is so important, and thankfully a replacement in many ways for conflict, the Welsh have continued their amazing feats, most recently through their soccer side.

There are still three Welsh fighting regiments: The Welsh Guards, The Royal Welch and the Queen's Dragoon Guards, and today we remember the First World War where many thousands of Welshmen gave up their lives for the United Kingdom.

The United Kingdom still feels it has an unique identity, as the recent referendum showed, but inevitably, many of us feel we have for centuries been affected by and are an integral part of Europe.

Wales looks set to remain an integral part of the United Kingdom, and does not seem to want to go its own way as Scotland may do but that does not detract from the patriotism the Welsh feel for their own country and which has made them fight to defend it.

Lightning Source UK Ltd.
Milton Keynes UK
UKOW04f0211230816

281233UK00001B/1/P